PERVASIVE PREVENTION

Advances in Criminology

Series Editor: David Nelken

Recent titles in the series

The full list of series titles can be found at the back of the book

Pervasive Prevention
A Feminist Reading of the Rise of the Security Society

TAMAR PITCH
University of Perugia, Italy

ASHGATE

Published by
Ashgate Publishing Limited
Wey Court East
Union Road
Farnham
Surrey, GU9 7PT
England

Ashgate Publishing Company
Suite 420
101 Cherry Street
Burlington
VT 05401-4405
USA

www.ashgate.com

British Library Cataloguing in Publication Data
Pitch, Tamar.
  Pervasive prevention : a feminist reading of the rise of
  the security society. — (Advances in criminology)
  1. Social control. 2. Risk—Sociological aspects.
  3. Precautionary principle. 4. Feminist theory.
  I. Title II. Series
  303.3'3-dc22

Library of Congress Cataloging-in-Publication Data
Pitch, Tamar.
  [Societ` della prevenzione. English]
  Pervasive prevention : a feminist reading of the rise of the security society / by Tamar Pitch.
       p. cm. — (Advances in criminology)
  Includes bibliographical references and index.
  ISBN 978-0-7546-7564-8 (hbk.) — ISBN 978-1-4094-0521-4 (ebook)
  1. Crime prevention—Social aspects. 2. Internal security—Social aspects. 3. Public safety—Social aspects. 4. Feminist theory. I. Title.
  HV7431.P53313 2009
  364.4—dc22

                                                                    2009052473

ISBN 9780754675648 (hbk)
ISBN 9781409405214 (ebk)

Mixed Sources
Product group from well-managed forests and other controlled sources
www.fsc.org Cert no. SA-COC-1565
© 1996 Forest Stewardship Council
FSC

Printed and bound in Great Britain by
MPG Books Group, UK

Contents

Foreword

It is a pleasure to introduce this insightful book by Tamar Pitch, a leading Italian writer on crime, law and feminism. Her latest volume offers a wide-ranging account of the centrality of prevention and offers a new way of looking at current changes in the configurations of western societies' obsession with the search for security and its often self-defeating results. She offers important and often caustic reminders of the futility of trying to treat dangers from others and the difficulties of building a just society as if this could be reduced to taking precautions against the risks of disease.

Pitch, writes, as she says, as one influenced by Italy, but what she has to tell us is not about Italy as such, even if her location outside the Anglo-American mainstream world of criminology sharpens her awareness of wider developments (the same goes for the works by Antonio Roversi and Alessandro De Giorgi already published in this series). Tamar Pitch is in fact an accomplished social theorist, and offers interesting commentary and adaptation of ideas taken from Beck, Bauman and others. But it is, above all, her feminist starting point that enables her to have a special perspective on what is happening. On the one hand the city is a place of opportunity for men, but of danger for women. Yet she sees the stress on prevention and self-control as a way to avoid risk as very much what women have always had to do – so in a sense the middle classes especially are engaged in a feminization of social control. She also stresses the role of women as victims (and the political costs of this limiting of their role) and the way they are used as an excuse in certain security campaigns. She relates her ideas to the latest thinking by David Garland, Jonathan Simon and Nikolas Rose – and behind them all sees Foucault's failure to theorize the implications of changes in social control for women and from a women's point of view. Her arguments are subtle and her ideas are not uncontroversial. She argues for example that new methods of seeking security seek liberation from bodies and ignore the awareness of 'the body' that women have, even though it could be objected that we live in a society that is obsessed with bodies. In any case, this and her other theses merit the wider debate which this translation into English will hopefully help them to achieve.

David Nelken
Series Editor

Preface

Perhaps the title of this small work is a bit pretentious. The issue of prevention, or rather the way in which the imperative of prevention has become so powerful and widespread today at all levels, merits a more profound discussion than I have presented here. I can only say that I could not resist the temptation to add my own definition of the contemporary social scenario in the so-called West to the many definitions already on the market. Furthermore, it is a definition which seems to me to be quite a comprehensive synthesis of the others.

This is my own reflection on questions that I confronted while working on the theme of urban safety, and, more generally, on social control today. This was certainly not the first time that I ran into 'prevention' in my studies of crime, its control, and related issues. In a certain sense, every study about deviance and social control sets out and proposes to figure out the causes of what has been variously labeled disorder, social disorganization, deviance, crime, and so on. And, in one way or another, this research into the underlying causes serves to or is used to try to prevent all these phenomena. For some years, however, and at least for about the last 20 years in Europe, certainly in Italy, the emphasis of studies and policies has shifted decisively from the problem of the 'producers' of disorder, disorganization, and crime, to studies of the victims, and especially the potential victims: in other words, all of us. And the meaning of prevention has also changed: prevention is for the most part intended today as every strategy and means to reduce the risk of victimization for all of us, while researches into the causes of 'social problems' have become outdated.

Risk, security – by now we are familiar with these themes as presented in political and scientific debate; but less so with prevention. Yet prevention is really what ties them together. It links them not only with regard to disorder and deviance, naturally, but to many other questions and problems as well. This work addresses how prevention intervenes in our daily lives, how this imperative has changed and in turn what changes it produces, as well as how the social scenario that was at the basis of research for social causes has also changed.

It will be clear that I made ample use of studies by many contemporary authors, trying to connect their various contributions, which I believe converge precisely on the topic of prevention. This, in addition to my attempt at a gendered reading of the question, constitutes perhaps the only originality this work purports to have.

Grateful acknowledgements are generally noted at this point. I believe that participating in the group of women we called *Balena* (which includes Maria Luisa Boccia, Gabriella Bonacchi, Maria Rosa Cutrufelli, Laura Gallucci, Marina Graziosi, Paola Masi, Bianca Pomeranzi and Rosetta Stella), and the passionate discussions that took place amongst us, beginning with the question of war, were fundamental for igniting the spark for many of the themes studied here. Later, I collaborated on the production of an issue of *DWF* (*DonnaWomenFemme*) on prevention with some of the women from this group, which not only spurred me to continue the research, but also provided me with essential guidance. I am also indebted to all of my friends from *Balena* for making a passionate and rich intellectual exchange possible – which is something precious and even essential in these times.

Maria Luisa Boccia and Ota De Leonardis read one section of this book, and I tried, as best I could, to follow some of their suggestions. I am aware of the fact that I did not reach the level of their expectations.

I am really grateful to Liza Tripp for her translation this book, certainly no easy job.

Janet MacMillan was more than an editor, and I wish to thank her for her precious advice and the great help she had given me to make this book more readable.

I dedicate this book to my son David, hoping that in the future I may dedicate to him a better one. Our life together often includes conflict, but it is always stimulating, and it is the context of my life, and therefore also that of my work.

Tamar Pitch

Introduction

I am a smoker, so I always feel guilty. But I don't want to (or perhaps I cannot) quit. So it was with pleasure, anxiety, and impatience that I heard the news that a hospital in Milan was equipped with a new machine capable of making a very precise early diagnosis of a variety of different tumours, including lung tumours. When this becomes available in Rome too, I'm sure I will make use of it immediately.

Moreover, I subject myself to an annual mammogram, Pap smear and periodic blood tests – despite two or three bad experiences when computer malfunctions falsely diagnosed me with illnesses I didn't have. I hardly use any animal fat anymore in meals, I make it a point of pride to buy 'organic' food, even if I have to spend time to search for it far from home, and even though it costs much more than the other kind, and I force my son to follow a Mediterranean diet. I go to the gym regularly and I insist that my son must also be involved in sports (of course I can do all of this because I have the time, and above all, adequate economic and cultural resources).

But this is not the end of it – a closer look reveals that the entirety of my daily life is marked by some kind of prevention. Often this happens unconsciously, routinely, but that doesn't make it any less restrictive. For example, when I think about it, I realize that I avoid certain places, certain hours and certain people in the city, and surely more than a man would in my situation.

Once, my partner ended up at the train station at two o'clock in the morning. There were no taxis, not to mention buses, so he calmly made his way home on foot. I would not have done that and I have often asked myself whether many women would have done so. I don't have daughters, but my friends that have admitted that they try to limit their freedom of movement more than they do with their sons, although even the latter are subjected to many more restrictions than we were when we were young.

Friendly encounters, and especially amorous ones, are subject to suspicion and mistrust. Sexuality, which for a brief period in the 1960s and 1970s was hailed as a form of liberty and creative expression, is now recast as a source of illness and contagion, if not abuse and violence. Encounters and sexuality, therefore, must be approached with caution, prudence and by putting a whole routine of prevention in motion against any possible harm they might cause.

If I lift my gaze when walking down the street or entering a bank or a shopping centre, I'm caught on closed-circuit televisions that monitor my movements, and in order for me to feel more secure they show that I'm in a supervised location where robbery, theft, molestation and other acts will be prevented or at least recorded. Access to many other zones in the city is controlled electronically this way, and for the same reason.

One could continue with many more examples. It is significant that two books that were written some time ago, one British and one American, are both entitled *The Culture of Fear*, thus presenting it as a given that our present condition is shaped by uncertainty and insecurity.

At the same time, we are encouraged to take risks, and to be ready for continual change, insecurity and flexibility. Many say that the past and the future tend to get gobbled up by a present that consists of unrelated and disconnected moments; a present that is not concerned with the future and purposefully ignores the past.

Connected with all of the above is the issue of a pressure towards individualization, a pressure that leaves us isolated, that thwarts the power of social connections, that puts forward biographical solutions to systemic problems and contradictions: an individualization that makes all of us individually responsible for anything that happens.

The horizon of certainty and stability has disintegrated in connection with what has come to be known as 'solid modernity' (to use an expression of Bauman's (2000). Marx noted earlier that his period was a time in which 'everything that is solid disappears into thin air') – or first modernity or modernity *tout court*, in contrast with postmodernity.[1] This disintegration is tied to the erosion of the state's power as the protector and source of generalized trust within a given territory. This produces an (illusory) new freedom for the individual – everything is in our hands – and, at the same time, a sense of being powerless to change the actual state of things. Indeed, change is tied to a project, or at least to a pull towards the future. Change is made possible by the recognition and analysis of the past and by the possibility for collective action based precisely on this project and recognition – all things that seem rather difficult, if not impossible, today.

---

1   Different ways of naming the period in which we live are, of course, not interchangeable. Each points to a different way of interpreting society, more or less in continuity with the past, and each uses different criteria and elements. The only thing they have in common is the sense of experiencing something that is at least partially new. I don't favor one over the other; indeed I wouldn't know how to say today which one is more appropriate. I use them synonymously, precisely to indicate what is new about what we confront.

We can interpret the imperative for private and individual prevention as a way to confront the anxiety and anguish associated with instability, loneliness, uncertainty, insecurity and widespread fears. It's a self-defeating imperative because, as we know, biographical solutions to systemic contradictions do not exist. In short, it's a labor of Sisyphus, which in and of itself contributes to perpetually reproducing the very conditions that create uncertainty and fear – in addition to making us feel guilty all the time and generating mistrust in our dealings with others.

But there are contradictions, at least apparently, between the widespread imperative for private prevention and other characteristics almost solely identified with our times. I will cite two: in the first place, prevention appears to be in contradiction to the demand that we take risks; secondly, prevention seems to signal a return to the horizon of foreseeable and controllable events, which many commentators conversely observe is disappearing with the disappearance of 'solid' modernity.

Furthermore, although it is true that the imperative for prevention is widely prevalent today, and, as I have said, has been privatized and individualized in accordance with changes attributed to our 'liquid modernity', there is, however, another level at which this plays out. Beyond modalities of self-control and self-surveillance, the imperative for prevention involves systematic and systematized control; a far cry perhaps from the Panoptic[2] model of solid modernity, but just as pervasive. This is the feature that orients, influences, sets the framework for and disciplines our everyday life – just as much if not more than ever before. However, it is less a form of thought-control than control over behaviour. Its reach encompasses entire populations, while notably targeting specific individuals. It's that all-present type of 'preventive' control that spreads through the use of electronic technology: credit cards, bank cards, electronics, closed-circuit TV cameras, computers, databases, and so on, right up to Big Brother satellites that are capable of recording what we do and say in our daily activities. The emphasis here is on controlling the future, predicting and directing it. The present is of interest only insofar as it provides data to prevent what would probably happen, based on simulations and statistical calculations.

The invasion of privacy has been a valid concern for some time already due to the development of electronic technologies for surveillance and control – or technology that is mainly used for that purpose. Indeed, as a result of this technology, the distinction between public and private spaces disappears. One of

---

2   I am referring here to Foucault's famous work on discipline as the heart of modernity; pervasive and widespread control, as well as self-control, are how the modern subject came into existence. The Panopticon, notoriously, is the structure designed by Jeremy Bentham, consisting of a circular tower in which an invisible guard can see yet not be seen by those he must control.

the characteristics of these methods of control is that they are even more invisible than the guard in the tall tower of the old Panopticon. These methods get mixed up with freedom because we are the ones who willingly use them. They do not lead back to a single, identifiable source of command (the state, for example). Instead, they are impersonal. They do not purvey ethical or even juridical values or norms. Control is achieved through an almost invisible modality of inclusion/exclusion. But perhaps the most important characteristic today is that they exert control and discipline beyond the territorial borders of a single state. Indeed, they are extraterritorial by definition, built for the cosmopolitan nomads that we have become, whether we wanted to or not.

Then there are those methods of more or less permanent repression and exclusion with which the process of economic globalization controls individuals and populations deemed 'expendable' (Bauman 2004) – refugee camps, temporary detention centres, etc., all of which fall outside the rule of law. And then there are the new procedures for border control, which were put in place to turn away the masses seeking a better way of life. The newest methods were first tailored for use in the United States to monitor 'presumed' terrorists. And, of course, there's the 'preventive war', which like a 'therapy' for a terminal disease – for example, interventions to excise cancers that wind up spreading – kills more healthy 'cells' than anything else.

The various ways of labelling present-day reality – the society of risk, information, surveillance, uncertainty – not only lead to various dystopian views, but also occasionally appear to be in conflict with each other even while the same themes are continually reappraised and shifted from one description to another. For example, the hypertrophy of the present appears to be negated by those who view the present as a prevailing attempt to influence the future (through information and surveillance). Also, how does one reconcile the process of individualization and privatization with a type of knowledge and administration based on probabilities, categories and actuarial tables?

Another important distinction must be put in evidence: the difference between descriptions that emphasize the presence of a tendency towards deresponsibilization (the disappearance of the real subject in its entirety and, above all, the disappearance of her life story, social identity and voice) on the one hand, and descriptions that instead emphasize a return to moral judgements to gain access to certain goods and services. The blaming of those that do not adopt certain precautions, as well as, in general, the emphasis on victimization, are an example of this, as we shall see. Are these differences incompatible with each other or is there a relationship and interrelationship between the various descriptions?

The question of how social control works today strikes me as particularly interesting. Some students talk about the worldwide extension of the Panopticon through expert systems of classification and categorization. Others put the emphasis on the fluid and factual, rather than the normative character of today's institutions. But those who speak of the extensive, global spread of a Panopticon forget an important aspect of the disciplinary function of the Panopticon itself: the internalization of control, the acting of domination through the 'minds' and 'consciousness' of those controlled, whereas the contemporary 'panopticon' works through systems that mainly target behaviours. Yet, anyone that denies that it's possible to speak of a Panopticon today has to come to terms not only with the use of sophisticated systems of classification and selection, but also with the internalization of attitudes and motivations for consumption, which many define as the ideology of contemporary capitalism, not to mention the imperative of independence, i.e., to be 'self-made', to take your life into your own hands and take responsibility for anything and everything that happens. This imperative has important moral implications, yet also seems to be in conflict with what others view as the dominant utilitarian ethic today.

Also, with regard to social control, what can we say about what has been called a new 'great internment', i.e., the growth of populations living under restrictive measures that limit their personal freedoms, whether they be, as I said, administrative measures (temporary detention centres) or judicial ones (prisons that long ago shed any pretence at rehabilitating inmates)?

One aspect that seems to be common to nearly every description available in the sociological marketplace today is the emphasis on the disappearance of not just 'society', an entity that probably eroded along with the nation state that gave birth to it, but of the social dimension itself as the concrete and symbolic fabric of relationships where individuals interact and by which they are motivated. Along with the social dimension, the past has also necessarily disappeared as a significant feature of life. The disagreements between the authors of different scenarios concern the dominance of the future over the present and vice versa, while there appears to be implicit agreement about the suppression and insignificance of the past in present times. The past, however, also means a relationship between cause and effect. The social causes that created the present are precisely what have disappeared from the scene. The type of prevention practiced today does not take 'causes' into account, and perhaps this is the biggest difference from the prevention of the past.

These are the things I want to talk about, and I maintain that using prevention as a lens may serve to clarify connections and differences since I think that prevention is directly implied by 'risk', 'information', and 'surveillance' and may be used to show how our everyday life is decided or 'channelled' by both our own individual efforts and by impersonal systems, both interacting in the name of 'prevention'.

In short, I would like to render explicit what appears implicit in many reflections on modernity today. A society of risk, a society of surveillance, a society of uncertainty, and cultures of fear imply both individualized modalities of action, and impersonal, collective modalities that are systematically geared for prevention. All these definitions simultaneously imply internalizing the moral imperative for self-sufficiency and independence and widely expanding plans for control of behaviours (rather than motivations). They imply policies that in the name of prevention favour seemingly 'soft' measures of control, as well as policies that are geared toward excluding, incapacitating, and neutralizing, still in the name of prevention.

However, this also requires questioning the things that are most commonly said about contemporaneity: that it has an unforeseeable and uncontrollable essence, that it is hypertrophic, that there is a widespread perception of powerlessness.

It also requires a gendered reading of this contemporaneity. Indeed it seems to me that while all of us are involved in 'preventing', the imperative of prevention is predominantly female gendered. This is both because it is traditionally women who take on the tasks of caring and concern themselves with prevention for the rest of the family, and because prevention is especially aimed at them. Men, on the other hand, are urged to take risks. And lastly, although this imperative puts every man and woman in the position of being a potential victim, this is a position and condition traditionally associated with the female sex.

Indeed, as I will try to show, women, and 'femaleness' more generally, also play a role of prime importance in the images of and justifications for contemporary wars, especially the so-called 'preventive' war.

The core of this work remains the question of social control. This is the key to reading other themes, as well as the main topic for our attention. Prevention appears to be at the centre of social control methods today. That is why I will give particular emphasis to those urban safety policies that have drawn a lot of attention in recent years, whether they are being planned or have already been put into action by local governments in the name of the citizens' right to be safe from the danger of becoming victims of common crime.[3]

---

3   This work is part of the Prin 2003 research project on *Analisi e valutazione delle politiche di sicurezza locale [Analysis and evaluation of local security policies]*. The empirical data I collected on local security as a problem of governance, which was co-financed by the University of Perugia, will be set forth in another volume. The contents presented here are more general reflections, which constitute the background.

Chapter 1
From One Modernity to the Next

Prevention and Progress

It should first be noted that prevention, by and large, is a good thing. If I dwell here to consider its, so to speak, dark sides, and the more or less unexpected consequences of its rhetorics and practices, that does not mean that prevention in and of itself is harmful. On the contrary, preventing events that would be harmful to oneself and the collectivity can only be considered useful and necessary. Moreover, this has in one form or another always been practised by human beings.

Today, however, we are witnessing two related phenomena: an intensification of the imperative of prevention, as well as its individualization and privatization. The origins and consequences of these two phenomena deserve examination because they shed light on our social life and its cultural and symbolic aspects, especially with regard to current modalities for social control.

There is nothing new about prevention, at least not on the surface. It became a slogan that spread with the first, so-called 'solid' modernity. Life expectancy growth in the wealthy Western world is certainly due to this. The rate of infant mortality and death in childbirth, for instance, was reduced from the time doctors began to wash their hands before operating. Not to mention vaccinations, which were adopted for mass use for soldiers during the First World War.

Prevention refers to an entire series of individual and social attitudes and practices that aim to reduce the probability that certain harmful events will occur. From this point of view, and from the point of view of controlling the present so that certain things don't happen in the future, prevention has always been practised in one form or another. Rites and myths of ancient societies and of so-called primitive societies provide abundant examples. It is no accident that Mary Douglas's research on the concept of pollution in 'traditional' societies led to her famous studies (Douglas 1966, 1985, 1992) on risk in contemporary society, which demonstrate that the denaturalization of events has a long history, perhaps as long as the existence of humanity. Attempts by humankind to prevent unwanted events are just as ancient. In Italy, the famous works by De Martino (1948, 1959) on the peasantry in the south during the 1940s and 1950s point to the rites that protected them from the extreme danger of losing their 'presence'.

What changed with (first) modernity are the instruments employed for these efforts and their corresponding ideology. Science played a central and key role here. It was necessary to have knowledge, in the scientific and positivist sense of the term, in order to control and prevent. Planning for the future was an integral part of the myth of progress. Projecting future society became a job of institutions, and of the state.

Even everyday life was directly involved, with the proliferation of the knowledge that invested it and aimed at changing it in order for it to acquire rationality, so that it was directed towards predetermined goals. The use of statistics to calculate not only the incidence of certain phenomena, but the probability that they will occur, became a common practice and extended to ever larger areas of social life.

The issues of hygiene and crime are perhaps the best examples of this. The discovery that bacteria can cause health problems led not only to the medical profession developing a cure, but also to the practice of cleanliness in the profession and the environment. Women played the leading role in this. The separation between public and private realms was supported by science with the rise of 'experts' for whom women became 'special clients or guinea pigs (Ehrenreich and English 1978). If middle-class women at the beginning of the nineteenth century suffered from the 'illness of emptiness' and were later diagnosed as hysterics, by entering into an alliance with experts they found a new role in domestic work. Domestic work became a full-time profession. The germ theory of disease necessitated cleanliness; the economy imposed the need for domestic efficiency.

It was in the second half of the nineteenth century that the work of middle-class women's organizations included reaching out to working-class and proletarian women to teach them how to clean their own homes and to take care of their own families' health. In a certain sense, prevention of illness in the course of everyday life became one of the instruments for the transmission and hegemony of bourgeois culture, and one of its key points was precisely the role of women, as wives and mothers, in taking care of the family and the proper reproduction of family members. The advice of experts and publicity about personal hygiene and homecare products played an important role at this time. This is how the role of wife and mother became, really and truly, a full-time job.

Indeed, the separation between internal and external realms, and taking care of the internal one – the home, the job of selecting, cleaning and so on – reflected, confirmed and reproduced the necessity for order and discipline in the outside world. The extent to which the question of order was involved in the rhetoric and acts of prevention will be clarified as we move on. (For a brilliant analysis of the relationship between oneself and the home, see Pasquinelli 2004.) Order, discipline, and the need for security acquired, as Foucault noted (1975), new form and substance with the emergence of modernity.

But prevention in everyday life – prevention by those with responsibility for housework – was certainly not limited to hygiene. Their primary responsibility was to see to their children's education, and this task was also what middle-class women taught and proselytized so that children found their way, became good workers and citizens that obeyed the law. Furthermore, women were to be good wives, to keep their husbands in line, to keep them from drinking too much, to see that they didn't go around making trouble. In short, it was women's work to see that men were ready and able and in good shape to report to work. Even today, women are generally blamed for men and children that turn out badly.

Beyond the good offices of wives and mothers, the prevention of common crime – of street crime – expressly became a task that the new criminology entrusted to research into the scientific causes of criminality itself. Since its birth as a scientific discipline, criminology adopted a positivist posture and never abandoned it until very recently. Yet it was the Italian positivist school more than any other that focused on prevention. Elaborating the concept of social dangerousness was crucial to the rise of the positivist school. Ferri (1979) was not only the first to conceive of punishment as a means of social defence, he also introduced the question of prevention to be achieved through reforms and social interventions, which were to take the various causes of crime into account in order to prevent crimes from happening.

The rise of fascism initially thwarted the widespread adoption of this approach in Italy. But it was picked up again and reformulated as a component of most of the studies on criminology and the literature on social control and deviance, on both sides of the Atlantic. The high point for this school of thought was the period when the welfare state was established and expanded.

On another level, Cesare Beccaria (2003) teaches that prevention is, of course, also an aim of the modern penal code insofar as the threat of punishment should serve to discourage criminal acts.

Urban planning too was very early on geared towards preventing disorder and the development of dangerous crowds. The grand boulevards in Paris supplanted back alleys, and Paris became the city of light partly in response to the Paris Commune of 1848. It is well known how much urban architecture implicitly or explicitly owes to the imperative of the prevention of disorder, crime, incivility and upheavals.

In short, prevention was an imperative and a central practice of modernity; it was then that social and other sciences emerged in order to understand the present for the purpose of controlling the future. All of this expert knowledge employed an etiological hypothesis. Once discovered the root causes of phenomena and what produced them in the past, it would be possible to prevent or control them in the future by intervening in those very causes. Time was ordered in a linear and progressive way, from the past to the future. The future, in a continuum with the past and the present, had a positive connotation. The future was going to be better than the past and the present, in part due to preventive measures. Faith in progress is indeed faith in the future; it is the projection of a promising future. In this way, prevention assumed the connotation of investing today for a better tomorrow – a bit like savings in macro and microeconomics. The causes of phenomena were traced not only to the 'natural' past, but also – indeed especially – to the social realm. More knowledge meant increased rationality in how to behave; more rationality signified improvement not only of physical conditions, but also of social and cultural ones.

After the Second World War, the establishment of welfare promised a secure future as a *right* for every man and woman through planning and social security, which everyone should contribute to through their work and the payment of taxes and contributions. Prevention here had a primarily social dimension because it was the state's responsibility and also because it was made possible through the 'solidarity' of citizens. The right to a home, the right to an education and the right to healthcare were key responsibilities of public institutions and an investment in the present to assure a better future.

Risks and Dangers

The distinction between risks and dangers differentiates between the possible consequences of a decision and the possible consequences of something that is beyond conscious human action. Natural catastrophes could then be described as dangers rather than risks. The pre-modern world would know of dangers rather than risks. But this distinction does not take into account that in the thinking and elaboration of many so-called primitive societies, natural catastrophes are, on the contrary, viewed as consequences of human actions. From this point of view, there really aren't dangers in these societies, but risks that must be prevented through special rituals and by strict and precise norms of life. In other words, social order can be seen as an all-encompassing modality for the prevention of risks.

The denaturalization of the world is not, as I said, a modern prerogative. Indeed, in different ways, it is a fundamental process of every human society. Similarly, prevention of risks is not a unique characteristic of a few societies, but a fundamental and structural trait of every society. What changes over space and time is what to prevent and how to do it, and the rhetoric used to justify prevention. Even in contemporary Western societies, some methods of risk prevention hark back to rituals that could be considered characteristic of pre-modern societies (so-called superstitious practices, for example).

The future is always uncertain and therefore at least partly portends risks. Rites, myths and religions are shields to face the future, when that future is, inevitably, death.

Mary Douglas (1966) said that religions in primitive societies are commonly characterized as religions of fear and terror, i.e., they are seen not only to generate terror, but are also viewed as themselves expressions of terror. Anthropologists, on the other hand, have not noted particular fears or terror in these societies, nor have they viewed their religions, at least in the way people lived and experienced them, as producing fear and terror. In sum, these societies are not different from ours. The impulse or the desire to make reality conform to an ideal of order is common to humans and cultures. It is disorder that is connoted as contamination, filth and terror, and it is order and disorder, or rather the way in which we view them, that differ in time and space. Misfortune and death are disorders and the fruit of disorder. Prevention is characterized here as the series of procedures put into motion to bring back, produce and maintain order. Prevention and control, and prevention and self-control are therefore interwoven.

The pressure towards self-control is stronger in modern societies where individualism is dominant. After all, self-control is the flip side, the more significant side, of social control in mass democratic societies, as was noted by G.H. Mead (1967). Foucault (1975) identifies the very production of individual subjectivity within disciplinary practices and devices. If this is how things are, the commonsensical opposition between freedom and control should be reconsidered. 'Modern' freedom is found precisely in self-control, and self-control, in turn, is exercised through innumerable forms of prevention geared to achieve security. We will return to this theme later.

Yet the social control of a traditional society is obtained through common norms that are internalized by everyone. As Durkheim (1989) said, the nucleus to be preserved, the supreme good that must be protected is here society itself, the 'community'. Therefore, self-control consists primarily of adhering to these norms, and order is lived and experienced as something eternal and unchangeable, something which has always been this way. The social control of a modern society, where the nucleus of internalized communal norms is restricted, is something quite different, and is represented by the protection of the individual. Here, the supreme good is one's own freedom. In modern society it is not as clear anymore what constitutes order, as order itself is the subject of change and transformation.

In so-called primitive or simple societies, the relationship between humans and non-humans is characterized in a different way than in modern society. Human and non-humans are closely intertwined, in the sense that there is not a rigid, defined boundary between what pertains to human beings and what belongs to the natural world. In 'primitive' societies, order is simultaneously natural and social;

the social order is the guarantee of the natural order, not only in the sense that it reflects it (it has to reflect it), but in the sense that it guarantees the natural order. A single transgression, which we might consider moral or social, can bring about natural catastrophes: death, earthquake, drought. This is where the demand for prevention comes from; prevention that in the first instance must restore order or ritualistically put it back into play.

In modern society, on the other hand, the non-human environment is external. It's a place to exercise human actions and is therefore subject to deliberate change as we shape it to our needs and desires. Human actions are liberated from their 'natural' limits, or what are considered to be such. In fact, limits are no longer even contemplated – everything is in our hands, both our individual and the collective destiny.

However, in extreme modernity or, as many refer to it, postmodernity, liquid modernity and so on, many of the elements of primitive societies seem to have returned. Knowledge of the often perverse consequences of scientific and technological progress, of the waste products of industrial society, along with the effects of the 'detraditionalization' and 'delocalization' produced by this particular mode of production, in short, the 'reflexivity' typical of this modernity, has further advanced the process of denaturalization. This has led to a perception of the relationship between humankind and nature that is in many ways very similar to that of primitive societies.

There are two differences: the question of boundaries is not posed as a given, but as the outcome of decisions and choices; the pressure towards taking risks typical of 'first' modernity is very much still with us. In brief, our society is a society of risk in two interconnected ways. As in primitive societies, there is the strong feeling that the way humans act with regard to the future, and to its risks and hazards, produces or may produce perverse and catastrophic consequences in the social and natural environment, which are themselves seen as involving each other and limiting each other. At the same time, as in the first modernity, the imperative to run risks remains and is even reinforced.

From this perspective, the drive toward practices and policies of prevention becomes pervasive and systematic, but concomitantly individualized and privatized. It takes the form of something that must or should be done to impede perverse consequences and at the same time as another risk to take.

In the following section, I will try to illustrate continuities and differences between modernity and extreme modernity.

Individualization, Insecurity, Freedom

The question of fear was central to the thinking and elaboration of modernity. If we understand modernity as the process of secularization, liberation from the bonds of ascribed status, limited social mobility, and established traditions, as well as the triumph of individual action and the emergence of the concept of the individual as ruler of his own life in the world, the corollary was precisely fear, uncertainty and distrust. Individual freedom and insecurity were intertwined from the start. Individual freedom takes the form of power, in the sense of one's power to do anything one wishes and to wish anything one wants. Personal identity was no longer defined by traditional belonging, but was instead defined by choice. Exchange, choice and contract became the basis of personal relationships.

After the shock of the American and French revolutions, some nineteenth-century theorists spoke of a shift from status to contract, from relatively stable relationships founded on being part of families, clans and associations, to relationships chosen on the basis of convenience, through a calculation of costs versus benefits.

The social sciences, beginning with sociology, were founded in the nineteenth century in order to enquire into the issue of order, of how to create 'society' in such a new world. From community to society, from mechanical solidarity to organic solidarity, this is how social evolution was traced by theorists such as Tönnies (1979) and Durkheim (1989). This is not to say that consistent evidence of social orders defined as communities and mechanical solidarity were not found to persist in contract societies. Yet, according to many, domination by the individual, and individualism, called for explicit policies to assure social cohesion, and these policies were necessarily informed by science, e.g. sociology.

These theories conflict with those according to which order was spontaneously generated through the action of self-interested individuals. The market, as the central arena in which to exercise these actions, would assure social order. Politics should only provide minimal conditions for the proper functioning of the market – e.g. merely the framework for peace and internal security – where economic transactions might take place.

Yet the reasoning behind both theories stems from a crucial event that had already occurred: the establishment of the modern state, the Leviathan as the monopoly of legitimate violence that defends individuals within the framework of certain 'rights' that an individual is 'naturally' entitled to – primarily, the right to life.

Castel (2003) speaks of two types of insecurity: external and internal. The first would have been dominant in the pre-modern era when the majority of threats were external – wars, invasions, illnesses. The second, conversely, prevailed in modern society, which was confronted with the emergence of the individual and the disintegration of family and social ties that constrained people in dependent and interdependent systems. Here, individual liberty was closely tied to widespread insecurity arising from the dissolution of alliances, loyalties, social relations and prior trust.

Thomas Hobbes (1996) was the major theorist of this insecurity – the cost of protection from insecurity was for him a pact of submission to sovereignty, an absolute power to which individuals sacrifice their natural liberty in exchange for the protection of their lives. For Hobbes, insecurity was innate to human beings, an anthropological trait linked to passions and desires that propel individuals into a battle of each against all. Agreement to submit to an absolute and sovereign authority was the only guarantee of peace and security. Internal security is precisely what we are talking about here, and for Hobbes this was the foundation and justification of the state. From this perspective, the state and positive law are to be seen as instruments for preventing the risks of inherently unlimited individual passions, which necessarily lead to the warfare of each against all. As Castel (2003: 14) says, it is 'in the shadow of the State as protector that modern man can freely cultivate his own personal vision and go forth to conquer nature, transforming it through his own labor and securing independence within his own properties'.

The description by Hobbes (1996) refers to a society in which individuals have broken the ties of primary belonging which conferred a certain level of (internal) security. The only truly efficacious response to widespread feelings of vulnerability and fragility in this type of society is the state's absolute power. Conversely, the liberal's minimal state (which is also the *gendarme* state or night watchman) concerns itself with securing internal public order while respecting individual freedom for its citizens. Its power to control and repress is therefore limited.

Therefore, in a state based on the rule of law, feelings of insecurity are necessarily endemic and cannot be eliminated. As Castel (2003) notes, there is a contradiction between a demand for absolute protection and an emphasis on rights when such a demand is produced by the very society of individuals which exhorts respect for the freedom and autonomy of all. Today, this emphasis takes the form of 'a recourse to law in every sphere of existence, including the most intimate and private' (Castel 2003: 23). The profound sense of insecurity in our society is rooted in this inextricable contradiction. 'Perhaps this is an intrinsic contradiction in the operation of modern democracy. It is expressed in the fact that security is a right, but this right cannot be fully respected without mobilizing the means that threaten this very right' (ibid. 24). Therefore, what flows from this is that demands for security threaten democracy itself.

While insecurity, or at least this type of insecurity, has to do with modernity and is inextricably tied to it, the state, and political action more broadly, were not however looked to as the sole means of protection.

This society, modern society, was animated by the rush into the future. The future, if governed and led in the right direction, could bring hope of a better life and general progress. Reason, as Hobbes himself argued, was seen as the driving force for the pursuit of peace (and therefore also for submission to absolute authority). In theory and practice, reason was called upon as the instrument to predict the future and prevent risks and dangers from occurring. There are two interrelated aspects to this: the search for political (and social) solutions, and the search for technical and scientific solutions. In reality, the two aspects are closely interwoven because the search for political responses became itself a science governed by the same criteria and principles of natural science. The sense of insecurity became the fundamental leaven for this research, insofar as it had to do with becoming and being individuals, and as such being able to control the world and themselves.

On the other hand, modern society celebrated risk. The very search for internal security and peace was due to the individuals' orientation towards the future, in which their life would be better. The great discoveries, voyages and conquests connoted modernity, as did the establishment of the state. The expansion of markets and the drive for personal enterprise in business, as well as the arts, speak of an epoch in which one must run risks, a time when one had to get a piece of the action, be daring, innovative and tempt fate. Fortune belongs to Man the Maker, according to a famous expression.

Yet all of this involves only half the population: men. It is men, indeed, that become individuals. They are the ones that subscribe to the social contract. They are the ones that free themselves from ascribed bonds and the ties of families, clans and associations. They are the ones who are supposed to run risks. This is not to say that the 'great transformation', as Polanyi (1957) calls it, the advent of industrial society, did not also involve women. Quite the contrary. By most accounts, women and children suffered the most from the perverse effects of this transformation.

Women did not, however, become citizens, or 'individuals' in the full sense of this word. For them the bonds of primary belonging were transformed but not dissolved. Carol Pateman (1988), borrowing from Freud, noted that the social contract was a contract between men, and which hid another contract – the sexual contract – that is, the domination of men over women, united in a pact among themselves. This is how the imperative to take risks was transformed for women into an imperative to avoid them. And those who couldn't – the large majority of poor women for whom the city meant poorhouses, workhouses, prostitution, servile labour – deserved what they had coming. 'Liberation' from traditional bonds was a condition of absolute danger for women, unless they belonged to someone (a man), insofar as they couldn't belong to themselves.

Locke (1987) theorized that private property is a means of protection in and of itself, as it provides autonomy and independence. Private property is not only ownership of goods and resources, but fundamentally self-ownership. This is coequal to individual liberty; it is what transforms individuals into citizens when they enter into the pact.

Women are not (generally) owners of property, neither of goods, nor resources, nor themselves. They continue to belong to their fathers and husbands. When the Rights of Man and the French Revolution burst on the political and social scene, the subjugation of women to their families, the separation of women from the public and political spheres and their relegation to the private sphere and the family were sanctioned. The rights and protections that men were accorded in their transactions stopped at the threshold of the home, which was discretionally ruled by the male head of the household. It is necessary, therefore, to reread modernity by taking into account that it held rather different prospects for men than for women.

If we take the city as the epitome of modernity,[1] it appears to be brimming with opportunities for men and with dangers for women. In the city, men are predators and women are the prey. At least this is how the city in industrial societies was depicted by novelists, journalists and thinkers throughout the nineteenth century. This is also how the city, and what it had to offer, was presented to women. Prudence and precaution were the watchwords for women, not audacity and enterprise. With regard to prevention, it was men's job to take risks by launching themselves into scientific innovations, economic enterprise and exploration because all these made it possible to harness the future, which, like nature, was to be dominated by humans, to be controlled, as well as explored. The job for women, on the other hand, completely revolved around putting prevention into practice for the purpose of taking care of and continually watching over themselves and their families, including the men. Taking care of the house and the family included, as I've said, important implications for prevention: domestic hygiene, caring for the boys and girls (so that the former didn't get involved in misdeeds and so the latter didn't get into trouble), and attentive care of husbands so that they were ready and able to go to the jobs that awaited them. These tasks were first enshrined as women's work in bourgeois families and then passed along to working-class families through teaching and proselytizing by upper-class women.

---

1   Regarding cities and fear, see the beautiful book by Marconi (2004), which traces the history of the city from medieval times to the present and how insecurities and fear were addressed with urban structures and modalities for construction and habitation.

The reverse is also true: women were dangerous to themselves and to men. They represented nature (which must be dominated), uncontrollable passion, chaos and disorder.

The issue of subjectivity is relevant here. To become an individual, you had to become your own master through a process of self-control, which is the other side of modern freedom. Foucault (1975) explains this very clearly, and Mead (1967) also underscores that self-control is the most significant exercise of social control in democratic societies. This modality of subjectivization was denied to women, and it is for this reason that they must be watched over: both in order to protect them from harm and to prevent the dangers they represented to men in general and to the symbolic and social order constructed by men.

Politics and Progress

Insecurity is said to be an inscribed condition of modernity. However, I repeat that insecurity in modernity fuelled actions aimed at the future. The goal of protection from danger and prevention of risks stimulated scientific research, which was guided by the idea of progress. Nature was not the only thing, however, that became an object for analysis and conquest. The 'social' also could and must be improved. Human nature, just like non-human nature, was now seen as something malleable, something that could be changed biologically as well as psychologically and socially.

We already said that the state is the institution that protects against internal threats to security, even though this is in contradiction to the concept of the rule of law, a contradiction that leads to virulent twists and turns in our so-called mature democracies, as we shall see.

The idea of progress, of a future that is always better than the past, is at the root both of revolutionary hypotheses and of social engineering and social reform. The emergence of new social actors on the public stage was cause for widespread fear as well as hope. The 'dangerous classes' were not only the wretched urban lumpen proletariat, but also the working masses that started to respond to the problems of their social insecurity by forming associations and mutual aid societies.

My point is that working-class struggles, turmoil and upheaval were simultaneously a symptom of widespread social insecurity as well as the cause of 'civil' insecurity for the bourgeois classes. The bourgeoisie's main solution was repression, unleashing a police state in the streets, plus the scientific study of deviance and crime. The working class's solution, on the other hand, was at the same time the idea of revolution and the practice of social reforms by forming trade unions and associations. Planning for the future, therefore, was the way in which both sides confronted misery, disorder, insecurity and fear.

The emergence of these dangerous classes was the indication that a police state was insufficient to guarantee internal peace, and that insecurity had something to do with danger to people and goods and that was coming from the living conditions of a market society . This implied running the risk of losing jobs, and therefore of wages. It also meant the risks to connected underemployment, inadequate salaries, old age, illness and disability. Castel (2003) calls this 'social insecurity'. From this point of view, the penal code, and the justice system in general, of a state based on the rule of law and guided by the purpose of 'general prevention' were wholly insufficient.

The creation of what became known after the Second World War as the welfare state was both a response to risks arising from the living conditions of a market society and a response to risks represented by the dangerous classes, in terms of crime as well as social and political conflicts. Without a doubt, the institutions of the welfare state were created during this period of conflict, and as an attempt by the ruling class to prevent and control it.

I already said that the natural and social sciences were the tools used to find an answer to insecurity. Science was intended as the tool for man's control over nature and the main way to foresee and prevent future risks by discovering the causes of current problems. Knowledge was intended primarily as the understanding of 'causes'. The past and the future were held together by a concatenation of cause and effect. Perverse effects could themselves be changed through greater knowledge.

Also social reform and even revolution could be planned by a scientific analysis based on an etiological paradigm: once the causes of something, anything, were identified, a solution would be found.

The institutions of the welfare state, including the trade unions and mass parties, provided another resource against insecurity: a new form of belonging, and thereby a social tie – one that was no longer ascribed but chosen. Moreover, by transforming the provisions of the welfare state into (social) rights, a new web of interdependence and reciprocity was delineated, which contributed to promoting new forms of solidarity in place of the traditional forms that were destroyed with the emergence of a market society. It was a process played out over two centuries, and did not become established everywhere (in the developed Western world) in the same way, at the same time, or by the same means. There were setbacks, intense conflicts, two World Wars, and the process was experienced differently by different groups and social classes. And this process never ceased to be the object of criticism and mistrust by 'conservative' and also 'progressive' forces.

I repeat that the ingredients were: faith in the future, in scientific, technological and social progress; the formation of horizontal solidarity (class, party and trade union) and vertical solidarity (the welfare state, civil rights); and external peace (in the last 50 years of the last century).

Prevention was seen as a goal and fundamental motor force for scientific research and social reform. The predominant modalities for implementing prevention policies were social, collective and public modalities especially in the last 50 years of the twentieth century. Institutions rather than individuals took responsibility for prevention, and they addressed risks that were considered social and public, such as illnesses. I do not mean to say by this that there was no pressure exerted on individuals to practice prevention. The predominant ethos, however, revolved around confronting risks that were collective and social and, therefore, public institutions, in the main, took responsibility for them.

Individual responsibility, in fact, remained in the background. The ultimate causes of dangerous phenomena were seen to be the workings of systems, apparatuses, structures and mechanisms in which the actions of individuals disappeared, and towards which individual action was felt as impotent.

Fear of the Future

In contrast with even 20 or 30 years ago, the imperative for prevention has not simply expanded, but it has also partially changed form. In the first place, faith in science and linear progress, trust in a more secure future, faith that scientific knowledge today can control and prevent the causes of harm that may manifest itself tomorrow, are in profound crisis. Indeed, the aberrant effects of science and technology are now perceived as particularly threatening and the reason for catastrophic risks. These perceptions meld into a 'community of anxiety' (Beck 1992). These perceptions are related to the effects of change and progress, also with regard to the relative risks of potentially taking control of and planning one's own life. Bauman (2005: 68) had the following to say about this:

> 'Progress', once the most extreme manifestation of radical optimism and a promise of universally shared and lasting happiness, has moved all the way to the opposite, dystopian and fatalistic pole of anticipation. It now stands for the threat of relentless and inescapable change that augurs not peace and respite but continuous crisis and strain, forbidding any moment of rest: a sort of game of musical chairs in which a second's inattention results in irreversible defeat and exclusion with no appeal allowed. Instead of great expectations and sweet dreams, 'progress' evokes an insomnia full of nightmares of 'being left behind', of missing the train or falling out of the window of a fast accelerating vehicle.

What changed and when did it happen?

In terms of science and technology, the atomic bomb was the watershed. Human beings invented something that could destroy the entire world and wipe out their own species. From that moment it was no longer possible to be naïve about scientific and technological progress. Yet, on another level, Benasayag and Schmit (2004) are right in defining the Shoah as the watershed. Indeed, the Shoah revealed the fallacy of faith in reason, of believing that reason could and certainly would lead humans to happiness, peace and prosperity. The genocide of the Jewish people was perpetrated in the heart of Europe, in civilized and cultured Germany, where 'reason' had its greatest resonance. From that point on, it became impossible to think of progress in terms of an enlightened journey – fuelled by reason – towards the greater good.

Ever-greater attention is today paid to the effects of our lifestyle and our mode of production on the environment. The question of the limits of development – that is the question of sustainable development – again ineluctably brings us back to the interwoven connections between the human species and nature today, just as it was, in other ways, in so-called primitive societies.

Exactly like in so-called primitive societies, (the consequences of) natural catastrophes are seen as strictly related to the way we live. They may not be immediately constructed as effects of 'moral' transgressions, but they are certainly seen as caused by decisions and choices which may appear political in the first analysis, yet fundamentally lead back to choices that contain moral aspects, in that they concern our values, aims, preferences and lifestyles. It took only two days for the shock of the recent catastrophic earthquake in Abruzzo to recede in order to give way to accusations, judicial investigations and general and specific blame: who's responsible for all those deaths? Politicians, constructors, engineers, city planners? And why did they act the way they acted: greed, ignorance, patronage?

This reflexive knowledge informs scientific research, be it in the so-called natural sciences or human and social sciences. There is no 'outside', nothing external to human action; no objects are independent of us (Latour 1999).

But the theme of 'outside', of the external, has another aspect to it as well: it is increasingly clear that it's impossible to export the negative consequences of our decisions and actions somewhere 'outside'. Acid rain and the tragedy of Chernobyl, for instance, show how the world has grown smaller. Something that occurs in one location has an impact in distant places and on distant people. If this is true for the environment, it is as true for every sector of human existence.[2]

---

2 There is a paradox here as well. In one way, the myth of progress has been demolished and faith in reason as the means to a better future suffers a vertical crisis.

Globalization and its effects have been widely defined, discussed and interpreted. As we know, the main processes underlying what is called 'globalization' have been under way for some centuries already, but what is perhaps typical of our times is the widespread personal experience of them, especially in terms of what Appadurai (1996) calls 'cultural contamination', e.g. the direct experience and therefore challenge of different ways of living, thinking, and self-perception. This can lead to more or less consciously questioning much that we have considered obvious and taken for granted – that background of trust in the world that allows us to go on without continually questioning every choice and decision we make, and that, more fundamentally, is the horizon of certainty for the events of everyday life. In many cases, this leads to an extremely defensive posture – an attempt to negate the validity of and even the existence of different values among us.

In the 1970s and early 1980s, a transformation of the organization of the workplace appeared, which was named post-Fordism. The neoliberal policies of Thatcher and Reagan provided the ideal framework for this transformation, supported it and legitimized it. The export of jobs, the introduction of flexibility and temporary work status, low-wage policies and unregulated worldwide circulation of capital were accompanied by the progressive demolition of the scaffolding of the welfare state. The dominant ideology preached individual responsibility, not to mention the privatization of services and resources that used to belong to the public. The end of the USSR and the return of war on the horizon of the Western world – moreover a new kind of war, where it was said that the 'enemy' could be anyone – contributed to creating a backdrop of widespread insecurity.

To get back to the topic of the preceding paragraphs, it was 'internal security', which never had a solid guarantee from the Rule of Law or the welfare state, that was once again felt to be the most consistent target of threats. Public security itself, along with 'civil' security was thrown into crisis. The guarantees of respect for rights and liberties were increasingly eroded by 'anti-terrorism' measures, but also, if less obviously, by surveillance equipment and omnipresent control, made possible thanks to new electronic technologies.

A society of risk, a society of uncertainty and insecurity, a culture of fear – these are the various ways that various authors have characterized our epoch. And, in any event, or perhaps for this very reason, the current rhetoric of prevention

---

In another way, however, the emphasis on science and technology has been intensified. Benasayag and Schmit (2004) highlight, for example, how this emphasis produces the sense that 'everything is possible', that there are no limits and therefore science and technology become autonomous of concrete social relations. But this is precisely the point: the vertiginous development of science and technology far exceeds our possibility to comprehend and make sense of their effects and possible consequences. Thus the sense that 'everything is possible' coexists with fear and a sense of powerlessness.

has markedly individualistic connotations, decisively shifting the emphasis of responsibility to the individual.

This brings us once again to the denaturalization of the world, which Mary Douglas (1992) spoke of with regard to traditional societies. We can state, very schematically, that up until recently this denaturalization involved research of what were undoubtedly human causes of events. Moreover, these causes were dealt with by collective human action. Responsibility for wrongs, damages, discomforts and misfortunes were mainly attributed to organizations, institutions and, of course, complex 'systems' that could only be confronted collectively and/or through other institutions, organizations and systems. Individual action was hidden, overshadowed or contained within the interaction of collective actors, whose roles were perceived to be predetermined. It could be said that social hypertrophy swallowed individual responsibility. The problem was always 'society', the 'system', 'capital', and so on.

The rhetoric is very different today. We always or almost always (with varying success) try to pin responsibility on indentified individuals for anything that happens.

> Of the different types of blaming systems that we can find in tribal society, the one we are in now is almost ready to treat every death as chargeable to someone's account, every accident as caused by someone's criminal negligence, every sickness as a threatened prosecution. Whose fault? is the first question. (Douglas 1992: 15–16)

On the one hand, we might welcome the individual actor's return on the social stage. But a price is paid for this reappearance: social and collective factors have disappeared or been overshadowed, and worse, all events that our own individual action can do nothing about are put into parentheses.

At least on a rhetorical level, it seems as if we have returned to early modernity, where the state as night watchman was limited to guaranteeing internal peace. As we shall see below, this is precisely the ultimate task assumed by the state and what it demands with greater force. But today, as in earlier times, there is a wide gap between reality and rhetoric, though the latter is important to our self-perception and how we live. Current economic and social conditions are created and guaranteed by the state and its institutions. Nevertheless, the erosion of welfare and the transition to post-Fordism also means that some of the institutions that guaranteed a certain type of belonging and solidarity – the mass parties and big trade unions – no longer provide this benefit. This is the context for the perception that one is alone, for the dissolution of transversal social ties, and why the sense of powerlessness is reinforced. To this we must add the shaking up of the traditional panorama of cities due to an immigration which, being very badly governed, produces distrust, fear and the sealing off of 'likeminded' people in ever-tighter circles.

The dominant neoliberal ideology insists on the one hand that being independent, autonomous and capable of taking care of oneself is the main civic virtue, and on the other that the only important bonds are the primary ones, e.g., the traditional family, even if the family itself has been eroded by the same economic and social processes that neoliberalism spawns.

In this context, prevention becomes a moral imperative connected with the civic virtue of self-reliance and individual responsibility. The crisis of the social institutions designed to create socialized and public prevention reinforces this imperative, and privatizes and individualizes it.

Gendered Prevention

Nowadays, the rhetoric of prevention is insistent about what we as individuals can and must do ourselves. We may be aware that the causes of an illness are (also) social. But the rhetoric of prevention insists on what individual men and women can do by themselves to prevent it.

For example, if we glance at the inserts tucked inside major newspapers, we will be struck by the amount of advice they offer on how to lead a life that is protected from all the most common illnesses by following a particular diet, a specific lifestyle, a regimen of physical exercise and much more. 'Green' magazines insist not only on 'ethical' consumption, but also health; that we should turn to 'safe' products and pay attention to the biological 'purity' of food. (More later, on the purity and the contextual consecration of what is 'natural'.)

There is also abundant advice to submit to periodic preventive medical examinations, which is especially directed to women, whose lives have always been subjected to medicalization more than those of men. Nowadays, this medicalization makes ample use of the vast new array of instruments for pathological examination. It starts with puberty: gynaecological and other examinations take place to make sure that everything is normal, and other examinations are needed in order to obtain the proper means of contraception (to prevent unwanted pregnancies, etc.). Then there's pregnancy: a veritable medical obstacle course. Continual blood tests, ultrasounds, amniocenteses, diets, pre-partum exercises and exercises to stay in shape have become practically obligatory. No woman really wants all this, but neither can she escape it. After all, this is presented as necessary not just for one's health, but for the future child's health, a future child perceived, due largely to these instruments and examinations, as autonomous from its mother's body, which in turn has been reduced to a mere container.

There is no doubt that death in childbirth and infant mortality have almost disappeared because of these practices, but at the cost of strictly disciplining the pregnancy and therefore the mother. Apart from medical scrutiny, pregnant women are subjected to often confusing and contradictory imperatives that concern their entire lifestyle: what, when and how to eat; what to avoid (cigarettes and alcohol, for example, to say nothing of other drug use); when and how long to sleep; how much and what kind of physical exercise they should do; and up to and including advice on what kind of music they should listen to (or have the foetus listen to), how to caress their belly, how to speak to the foetus, and so on. All this has the connotation of a moral imperative. If you don't do some of these things, or if you do things that you're advised not to, or that are prohibited, you feel guilty. Any woman that cannot follow such a rigidly disciplined lifestyle – work obligations, other children to look after – will probably live uneasily during her pregnancy. One becomes a potentially 'bad' mother during pregnancy. No matter what happens to the child in the years ahead, thoughts will often be cast back to what should have been done during the pregnancy that was or was not done. Now there is even the real possibility of being brought to trial by one's own children, as has happened in the US, for what was or wasn't done when the mother was pregnant.

Then there are the periodic examinations for cervical cancer (the Pap test), breast and ovarian ultrasound, and mammograms; not to mention therapies for menopause, in order to prevent osteoporosis and other evils. These are all good things, of course, and when we can, and to the degree we can, we willingly undergo these procedures. The point, which will be elaborated below, is that these preventive measures are not available to everyone. The imperative to take care of oneself is universal, but the means to do so are not. And it is not only a question of economic resources, but also of cultural ones. Proper education and the ability to understand and interpret health advice are as important.

Hygiene is an imperative first and foremost for the home. Advertisements for detergents show small children playing on the ground and emphasize the power of detergents to destroy bacteria that lurk in dirt. Garments for newborns of course require proper sterilization. 'Dirt' from children that play on the sidewalk and from garments, tableware and the very environments in which we live is the object of intense advertising campaigns directed primarily at women. And of course, what is considered 'dirty' today is not what was considered dirty only 40 years ago: 'dirt' expands with the development of gadgets and materials that are supposed to do away with it. And, as usual, 'dirt' takes on the symbolic value of impurity, contamination: 'dirt' connotes disorder, the threat of an ungovernable world.

I stress that it is primarily women who bear the burden of prevention, even more than before, for themselves and their families, because this point strikes me as decisive. On the one hand, the imperative to run risks is still geared more towards men than women; the latter are saddled with the opposite principle of prevention. But on the other hand, policies for prevention imposed on women constitute another form of social control over them and others, which again, even more than before, constitutes most of the domestic labour and care that is delegated to women.

There is also another important aspect to this that should be kept in mind: the question of order itself. Cleanliness, sterilization, environmental and home hygiene lead back, as was said above, to the symbolic imperative to restore order to a world of confusion which is threatened by contamination. In this sense, disorder alludes to social disorder, to the loss of identity and to the blurring of boundaries between the world outside and oneself. So, women are entrusted, more or less explicitly, with a fundamental task: to hold together or reconstruct a familiar and trustworthy world (Pasquinelli 2004).

It is in this context that we have to interpret the command to women to take good care of themselves so that their own bodies are safe, sound, secure. The female body, relatively speaking, is among those bodies that remain visible as such, whereas, as we shall see, 'bodies' tend to disappear. Women must maintain its integrity, not for themselves, but, as in the past, for others. Women's bodies allude not only to reproduction of the species, but also to the continuity of 'family', 'nation', 'ethnic group', 'national identity' and 'tradition'. From this point of view, it is women themselves who are considered a risk, or better yet, a danger. Women are dangerous for the social and symbolic order. It is their bodies, therefore, that must be strictly disciplined and controlled.

The Security Market

It is striking how many advertising products today exploit the issue of safety and security. Automobiles, domestic appliances, and of course all those gadgets designed specifically for security – household alarms for the elderly, anti-theft devices for cars and homes, smoke alarms and detectors for gas leaks – plus the huge insurance market.

Security has become both a product and a way to sell products, transmitting the imperative to prevent risks and protect individuals from harm, while disseminating a culture of suspicion and fear. There is a specific market for security today, including exhibits:

> Securebuilding is the security sector within the Saiedue Living display on view from today until March 21 at the Bologna fair, an area where solutions for a more secure home will be presented. All the new products designed to increase building security will also be shown in a catalogue. (*La Repubblica*, 17 March 2004: 25)

Italy has recorded a boom in sales of security devices, yet still lags behind the sales registered in other European countries and in the United States. Home alarm systems have the greatest market share and they are often either promoted or suggested by local councils. The town of Brescia exhorts: equip the door to your house with appropriate security devices, bulletproof the door, add a second lock, and install an alarm system. 'This was a handbook sponsored by Megaitalia, a company that makes security systems, explained Paolo Corsini, the Democrats of the Left mayor of Brescia' (*La Repubblica*, 17 March 2004: 13).

As Bauman noted (2005: 69): 'A lot of commercial capital can be garnered from insecurity and fear – and it is.' He recounts the increased sales of SUVs, thanks to advertisements that deliberately exploit 'fears of catastrophic terrorism'.

Security policies will be addressed in another chapter. Here I only wish to note the growing significance of the private market for security and prevention; a market that obviously demands publicity and enjoys state support. At the same time, it seems obvious that if everybody has to take care of themselves, not everybody can afford it.

The society of risk, as Beck (1992) said, is the society that instead of distributing goods, distributes evils. Hierarchies and inequalities are reproduced and reinforced through this distribution. One may add that bad things are doled out especially to those that can't do anything to prevent them, as all that must be done, must be done by individuals with their own resources.

The Threat of Violence Extends Everywhere

In the first place, the push to make everyone responsible for their own care has laden us with enormous responsibilities. One of the effects is to shift our attention to what we can individually (presumably) prevent, rather than to the social and environmental context, which cannot be confronted by one lone individual.

> We are engrossed in spying out the 'seven signs of cancer' or 'the five symptoms of depression', or in exorcising the spectre of high blood pressure and high cholesterol, stress and obesity. In other words, we seek substitute targets on which to unload the surplus fear that has been barred from its natural outlets, and find such makeshifts in taking elaborate precautions against cigarette smoke, obesity, fast food, unprotected sex or exposure to the sun. (Bauman 2005: 69)

Another effect, as I have said repeatedly above, is a kind of continual self-surveillance, which is a ponderous discipline in our daily lives.

Isolation is an even more evident effect. We are exhorted to be cautious when meeting others as we must do everything possible to prevent harm to ourselves or to our loved ones. In the last 20 years, together with the repeated rigmarole about the necessity and of course the intrinsic moral virtue of independence and autonomy, we have been subjected to one campaign after another denouncing child abuse, the criminality of immigrants, sexual harassment at the workplace, so-called 'mobbing', and now *bullismo* [bullying] (which once upon a time we used to regard as 'normal' conflict between classmates at school). These phenomena should certainly not be underestimated. Sexual harassment in particular had until recently been overlooked for what it is, that is a powerful means to curb women's work careers. Simultaneously and inevitably, these campaigns generated a climate of suspicion that often led to the wrong targets. So-called paedophilia, in fact, is much more prevalent within the safe confines of the home than at the hands of treacherous and dark-skinned immigrants; violent crime is perpetrated far more by Italians than foreigners, etc.

It is our entire everyday life that is being denounced as risky and dangerous. Let's take sex, for instance: while in the 1960s and early 1970s sex and sexuality were extolled as prime sites for self-expression and happiness, nowadays they are talked about only as sources of violence, harm and illness. Feminist campaigns against rape no doubt unintentionally contributed to this new climate. While they succeeded in revealing the violence in male attitudes and behaviours which until then had been perceived as 'normal', they also spread the (normative) ideal that non-violent sex is only that which is consummated between 'equals' through affection and 'tenderness', thereby excluding any other way of practising and expressing sexuality. The campaign against child sexual abuse had such an inflammatory tenor that several people were prosecuted – male and female schoolteachers, and of course fathers and mothers (accusations of child sexual abuse by one of the partners appears to have become a standard move in the conflict between separating or divorcing parents) – and later were revealed to be unfounded. Fear of AIDS took care of the rest, together with the ever-expanding notion of sexual harassment, which led to the drafting and full-scale adoption of behavioural codes by companies and in the workplace in general. The widening fear of date rape, i.e., rape by a lover on a date, led one American critic to denounce the present climate as closely resembling that of the Victorian era. In Italy, on the other hand, we appear to be back to colonial times, as those who are feared as sexually potent, aggressive and voracious are dark(er)-skinned migrants.

The construction of sexual relationships as intrinsically dangerous contributes to the diffuse fear, suspicion and distrust of strangers. This suspicion leads to a retreat to what is constructed as the only secure refuge: one's home, family, friends. Yet, as many women who have been victims of partner's or family members' violence well know, this is mainly a false picture, also belied by the growing number of homicides and rapes of women by abandoned fiancées and ex-husbands.

Some years ago, a six-year-old child was suspended from an American elementary school for kissing a classmate without first asking her permission. Children are under ever-closer surveillance and their freedom of movement and playtime is curtailed, not to mention their relationships with adults who are not part of the family's intimate circle, with the result being to deprive them of the possibility of developing their own autonomy and self-confidence.

Victims

All that was said above has to do with the centrality and relevance attributed to victimization and to victims. Each and every one of us is reconstructed as a potential or actual victim of something or other.

The notion of victim has these characteristics, distinguishing it from that of 'oppressed': one is a victim of someone or something that is easily identifiable, and to which it is possible to attribute responsibility for our victimization. One is a victim for having suffered a clear and measurable harm, rather than for having suffered the widespread effects of a generalized condition. We can all of us be or become victims, regardless of our social, economic or cultural status, or the sex to which we belong. We are, or become, victims usually because of a definite act, delimited in time and space; victimization is, in short, more an event than a characteristic that involves our entire biography.

Victimization alludes to a condition of vulnerability and weakness that was at one time reserved to women (and to children and the elderly), but which has now become generalized. It is a condition that becomes the premise for assuming 'voice', which legitimizes protest, at least collective protest, with the evident paradox that empowerment seems to be strictly connected to vulnerability and weakness. In order to be able to speak, protest, act against and along with others, it is, in short, necessary to reconstruct oneself as the victim of someone or something. This leads to competition with other victims of someone or something else, a competition of who is the more victimized and the most deserving, because to be a deserving victim, a 'real' victim, it is not enough to have suffered something from someone. One must also have done everything possible not to be victimized, or be able to demonstrate that one was not in a position to have been able to do anything to avoid it.

What keeps together groups of victims is the often accidental fact of having suffered the same type of harm (for example, being relatives of people killed by drunk drivers), not that of sharing a more complex life condition. This leads them to actions and requests which are themselves also definite, generally temporary when they are not ephemeral, and directed towards a single objective or against a single target. In this they differ from aggregations based on assuming the status of the 'oppressed' and 'exploited' individuals. Bauman (1999) speaks about 'communities of accomplices' to indicate those aggregations of citizens that are formed on the basis of the fear of something or to avoid something else: aggregations based on the self-attribution of the status of victim are usually exactly of this type. While some have been shown to be less ephemeral and capable of sustained political action over time, in general they are characterized by having a sole and well-identified objective.

In Italy, we are familiar with many groups of this type: all of the relatives of victims of something (of the Mafia, terrorism, mental illness), as well as aggregations of citizens that join together to prevent, e.g., the installation of gypsy camps, the practice of street prostitution, the entry of migrants into their neighbourhood (the Italian variety of Nimby groups). What unites them is mistrust and fear rather than reciprocal trust and, as a rule, precisely because of this it is not trust, at least not generalized trust, that is produced by them. The current rhetorics of prevention make extensive use of the category of victim, whether actual or potential, and of the risks of victimization. Individualization, on the one hand, and privatization, on the other, are corollaries.

By individualization I mean, as I already said, shifting the entire responsibility for prevention to the individual. Privatization on the other hand indicates the result of those processes whereby what until very recently was the task of public institutions is shifted not just to be the individual's responsibility but handed out to the market and/or the so-called third sector. Privatization can occur in various ways: directly, by putting services and resources that were previously provided by the state on the market, or indirectly, by externalizing skills, providing financing for services and resources to private entities, or even through contractualization, that is negotiation of a contractual kind between various entities, both public and private, in order to produce and distribute a certain resource (for example, local contracts for urban safety policies).

Individualization and privatization are closely interrelated, and in turn depend on the decline (or transformation) of welfare institutions and culture. Both refer to a rhetoric that extols personal autonomy and independence (in addition to efficiency) as virtues that are not only private, but also public – civic. In this day and age, a good citizen is one who does not depend on others, and especially one who does not depend on the 'state', its services, its resources and provisions. Personal autonomy, the capacity and opportunity to make choices, plans, to set one's own standards of behaviour, is seen as the same as 'independence', in the literal sense of the word: self-sufficiency, not needing help or assistance from others, nor, of course, being dependent on 'things' (medication, alcohol, tobacco, drugs).

The reality, naturally, is much different. We all depend on others, and on things of various kinds: social ties are ties of reciprocal interdependence, even if the ties of personal dependence have been diminishing since modernity. And autonomy is not and cannot be a function of independence: it depends both on possessing the adequate economic, social and cultural resources and on having and using affective resources and social ties (what is today called 'social capital'). Both types of resources have something to do with interdependence.

There's more: in the condition of advanced modernity, as Beck calls it, 'individualization takes place under the general conditions of a societalizing process that makes individual autonomizations increasingly impossible. The individual is indeed removed from traditional commitments and support relationships, but exchanges them for the constraints of existence in the labor market and as a consumer ... The place of *traditional* ties and social forms ... is taken up by *secondary* agencies and institutions, which stamp the biography' of the individual and make that person dependent upon fashions, social policy, economic cycles and markets, contrary to the image of individual control which establishes itself in consciousness (Beck 1992: 131). Therefore, the cultural pressure for independence is contradicted by the growing and ineradicable dependency of each person on conditions and situations that are well beyond the scope of individual action.

Paradoxically, the rhetorics of independence are often found in discourses aimed at convincing people that it is necessary to rely on experts to achieve actual independence. This does not only concern cases related to substance dependencies – with respect to which, among other things, one of the most advised treatment regimens is entering closed communities where there is iron discipline and personal dependence on a charismatic figure – but issues relating to relations in daily life that are incessantly reconstructed as psychological problems. Loving too much or not being able to love, eating too much or too little, being too severe or not severe enough with one's children, having too many or too few friends, having too much or too little ambition.

Being at ease with oneself, a slogan that dates back to at least the 1960s, in reality seems to be the result of a complicated and very demanding task which needs experts to be achieved and experts to define its actual composition. Many New Age practices don't depart very much from 'scientific' knowledge – at least in the justifications and functions – through which one seeks to direct one's individual life towards 'self-realization', a term which is to say the least rather mysterious, and by which a variety of things is meant, independence always included among them. Expert, usually psychological, knowledge, New Age practices, philosophies, religions and practices of Eastern origin should allow us to assume full control of our minds and bodies, to be responsible for ourselves, to concentrate on our own well-being. A major daily recently featured a new type of psychology service, said to be positive, that proposes preventing bad moods and possible descents into sadness. But, as Ehrenreich and English (1979: 304) were already keenly noting in 1978:

> If you are not responsible to anyone but yourself, it follows that relationships with other people are merely there to be exploited when (emotionally) profitable and terminated when they cease to be profitable. The primary assumption is that each person in a relationship has a set of emotional, sexual, or other 'needs' which he or she wants met. If they are no longer being satisfied by a friend or sexual partner, then that bond may be broken just as reasonably as a buyer could take his business away from a seller if he found a better price.

Hence the contradictoriness I already noted, between the rhetoric of do-it-yourself and the often complementary idea of traditional values with respect to family.

In turn, Benasayag and Schmit (2004: 130) bring to light a pressure for individual autonomy that in reality is comprised of 'force' and domination. They say that one who dominates is free: 'Our contemporaries dream of autonomy-domination, they aspire to conquer power over others and over the environment that allows them to pursue their own desires, without obstacles and without opposition from anyone.' This leads 'to a theory and a psychotherapeutic practice of control and command, which in the jargon we call the "psychology of a strong me"' (ibid. 130). The autonomy-domination exhorted casts a light of suspicion over all ties, especially when the individual at the centre of them is 'weak' (that is, has scarce resources, both economic and social, and cultural and psychological) and it reconstructs them as 'dependencies' from which it is necessary to free oneself.

What is rarely brought to light, in this as in other treatments, is the profoundly male nature of such a conception, in which, precisely, one becomes a whole individual only when one does not have ties, or can put them between parentheses or, better yet, dominate them. And complementarily, the scorn and status of lasting civil and moral inferiority attributed to whoever, but as a general rule women, cannot or does not want to understand relationships in this way.

Relationships, feminism says, form us, make us what we are without, however, us necessarily being determined by them. The issue is not freeing oneself from ties, but recognizing them, making them our own, using them as a point of departure. What follows then is a very different conception of autonomy, understood as the situation of one who can choose how to be and what to become starting from what one is, including obviously those ties that make one what one is, first of all one's own body and one's own sex. And, in this sense, individual autonomy requires others and other things, that is, economic, social and cultural resources along with strong and significant relationships.

If the male conception of moral and civil individuality is certainly not new, but emerged, as previously stated, with modernity, then today's emphasis on responsibility, autonomy, independence, along with the decline in welfare culture and institutions, exacerbates and reinforces it.

Many years ago, Lasch (1979) called our culture one of narcissism, a culture of retreating into oneself and at the same time, and complementarily, fleeing from the care of others and the care of common goods. However, it seems to me that narcissism is only one form, or perhaps one result, of the attempt, exhorted as a moral imperative, to defeat all those forces that are construed as being sinister and which try to prevent us from independence and autonomy. In this sense, rather than being narcissistic, our culture is one of fear. And in fact it is to fear that the notion of victimization refers; fear connotes the nerve-wracking search for security and preventive control over one's own future, and it is fear that is used, in various ways, within the rhetorics of prevention.

The contemporary centrality of the rhetoric of victimization has other effects too: 'victims' have acquired an important voice with respect to the direction of criminal and penitentiary policies. Somewhat diametrically opposed examples are the introduction of the institution of penal mediation, in Italy in juvenile criminal procedure, but in other countries also for adults, and the influence of the crime victims' lobbies in the United States for policies like 'three strikes and you're out' (Re 2006). Both have the objective of eliminating recidivism, but the former, informed by the principles of re-education and the responsibility of the offender, is dripping with moral references, while the latter is purely neutralizing, inspired instead by 'vengeful' motivations, geared towards forever excluding the offender from civil life. In short, we appear to have returned to a privatized conception of criminal justice, where what counts first of all is the satisfaction of the demands of the victims – those particular victims – rather than the imperative of general prevention and respect of the guarantees of the accused and offender.

As we will see, the policies geared towards producing security also have as an objective and as justification the sheltering of all of us – potential victims – from the risks of common crime. The new centrality of victims displaces the axis of criminal justice from a prevention of crimes that relied on the threat of penalty directed towards all citizens, to a prevention that relies on measures of surveillance, sterilization of a territory and the neutralization of offenders.

Time

The condition of insecurity and generalized uncertainty in which we all live is the hidden and perverse side of the pressure for autonomy and, especially, for independence. Passed off as increased individual freedom, the push towards self-control and the control of our life's circumstances (on those we think we might have an impact) proves to be a consistent and incessant running on empty, confronting more and more risks and more and more enemies, in an attempt to find 'biographical solutions to systemic contradictions' (Beck 1992). One is, as Castel says (2003), *obligated to be free*, because the rhetorics of prevention are indeed constructed around a paradox: do-it-yourself, independence, the 'freedom' to be and do whatever one wants, even to take risks. Today, hegemonic public discourse emphasizes, at the same time and apparently contradictorily, both the need and the intrinsic virtue of taking risks, above all in the economic sphere and in the market, and the need and the intrinsic virtue of adopting a precautionary behaviour and attitude aimed at preventing these same risks.

What explicitly combines these two opposing imperatives is that both are directed at the individual person and urge that person to be competent or acquire competence, but there is something else that connects them more subtly. On the face of it, taking risks opens up the future, while prevention seeks to shape and control it. But the risks that must be taken are precisely what make the future threatening, at least for most of us. Indeed, betting on futures, playing the stock market, making capital investments are for very few people. (It is so true that when people take such risks, many, as has recently happened, lose ruinously. Shortly before the major crisis of 1929, someone said that when even one's own driver starts playing the stock market, then the time has come to pull out.) For others, taking risks means flexibility in work, precariousness, forced nomadism – in a word, an uncertainty and an insecurity that are not open to the future, but lead to fearing it: prevention is thus closely connected with risk-taking; it's the other side of it.

We may then agree with those who say, about our time, that there is a hypertrophy of the present since risk-taking refers to the present, just as prevention is a practice that occurs in the present. Actually, I think that both refer to a *threatening* future, and that the present is instead lived as a function of this threat. Risk-taking involves prevention, and both are directed at the future – although not happily and trustfully, but with fear and dread.

> The center of risk consciousness lies not in the present, *but in the future*. In the risk society the past loses the power to determine the present. Its place is taken by the future, thus something non-existent, invented, fictive as the 'cause' of current experience and action. We become active today to prevent, alleviate or take precautions against the problems of tomorrow and the day after tomorrow – or not to do so. (Beck 1992: 34)

If this does not seem very different from what happened in the past, the difference is in the fact that the future expected is not one of hope and progress, but one rife with threats. The action that this causes is an action aimed at preventing harm, in the sense that it seems entirely directed towards this purpose, rather than being directed not only at this, but also, and complementarily, at producing a better future. The unpredictability of the future, in short, is no longer a mixture of hopes and threats, but a mass of threats alone.

Action is 'caused' by the (threatening) future in another sense as well: as Beck indeed indicates, one no longer seems to act on the basis of their own past; if we intend the past, which is at the root of present problems which might be changed through appropriate actions, to influence the future then we need to know it in its status as the cause of present problems. The idea of progress and hope in the future were condensed into this: knowing the (past) causes of ills meant having or being able to have the tools to prevent and correct them in the future. Past, present and future were experienced as connected by a causal chain.

I don't mean to say that today the idea of 'cause' has disappeared; that would be an absurdity. However, what has come undone, even in the usual meaning, is the idea of a simple linearity of cause and effect, or the faith in an absolute and transparent rationality, which would allow the 'cause' to not only be identified but also eliminated. Instead what come to light, even more so than before, are the perverse consequences of every attempt to come to terms with 'causes' and the inextricable tie between 'solution' and 'problem', as well as the illusoriness of an absolute rationality. This contributes to making the past insignificant. Furthermore, the speed of change has become increasingly rapid; the present becomes the past in a second and nullifies it.

The past, therefore, has disappeared. It is not from the past, not even one's own, that resources and knowledge can be drawn in order to face the present and future. The past vanishes immediately; it does not project meanings onto the present; it does not give sense to it. Personal lives tend to occur in discontinuity; they have become puzzles that perhaps only someone from the outside, or later when we are no longer here, will be able to give some sense to.

Sociologists talk about detraditionalization; they and the postmodern philosophers celebrate discontinuity as the freedom to try on countless different identities, or even as a way to once and for all destroy the very concept of identity. The rhetorics of the market encourage continuous change, both in products and in their consumption and use.

At the same time, and by no coincidence, conflicts to affirm identity and more or less reinvented traditions multiply and become cruel; differences, eminently relational concepts, are absolutized, rigidly parametered, changed into ethnicities and 'cultures' that are understood as being in and of themselves whole and pure. It is no coincidence, because these are moves to defensively reconquer a past, a past that does not only give meaning and continuity to the present and to the future, but wants them to be strictly linked to it.

> The scenario of a widespread uprootedness, an eternal present, in which the known references disappear, to which the flow of mass-media communication has made its decisive contribution, has conversely had as its counterpart the emergence and proliferation of neonationalism, ethnicism, fundamentalism, exclusive citizenships and chauvinists. A void was opened, that void was filled and the needs of identity found new paths to be satisfied. The identity-making casting and closures were nourished by invented traditions, thereby proposing a different relationship with the past. (Gallerano 1999: 8)

Thus these are defensive moves, and presumably losing ones, but which bear witness to that function of the past which consists of anchorage in a place and a situation, an anchorage that allows and indeed aids the leap towards the future, the trip to the unknown, since one thinks one knows who one is and from where one comes. I recall a Kafka quote on this, where he says that in order to leave one needs to have really lived and experienced what is being left.

There is, however, a difference between travel and nomadism. It is possible for travel not to have a direction or a precise purpose, but connotes a trajectory that departs from a particular location, from, in short, a departure point which marks a before and after. However more intimately the departure point is known, all the more rich the trip will be. Travel is thus directed movement, plan and process together, while nomadism is a life condition which does not provide a before and after. Travel represents a leap towards the future, while nomadism seems to occur in an eternal present. In travel one takes risks, one gets in the game, one is pushed by curiosity towards otherness. The nomad brings with him everything he has, while the traveller leaves behind what she knows, the security of the already known.

From this viewpoint, perhaps the only true travellers today are migrants on a path towards the (almost) unknown in the hopes of a better future. For them, there is a past. And perhaps that is why, having a very concrete past, they also seem to have a body, which we, by no coincidence, fear.

Bodies

The current disappearance of the body seems to me to be a metaphor, figure and 'cause' of a nomadism that may not have anything to do with true and actual movement. It is instead a psychic nomadism, where what comes to be missing is precisely the origin, the point of departure, the concrete location in an intimately known past which is made one's own.

The body is disappearing in many ways: in virtual communication; in the deconstruction activated by surveillance technologies, where what counts are the traces, the signs; in the decomposition and recomposition carried out in organ transplants (recently there was news of a face transplant); in medically assisted procreation, where sexuality disappears along with bodies; in genetic research; in the prevalence that investigative techniques that rely on profiling are assuming. Bodies are disappearing in their entirety, in their concreteness. We can apparently no longer rely on them for identifying ourselves, placing ourselves, recognizing ourselves.

There are two types of processes leading to the disappearance of bodies: on the one hand, an extreme denaturalization that occurs with technologies of communication; on the other hand an extreme renaturalization, the (apparent) reduction to pure biological data that occurs with transplants, genetic research technologies, profiling and so on. Our bodies, until now, were an inseparable mix of nature and culture, biology and history, social and individual, and therefore they were and are means for relationships and reciprocal recognition. The disappearance of the body goes along with the parenthesizing of the past, the decline of the social and the imperative to free oneself from ties.

> It is often said that we are our own genes, that we are our own information. We thus give in to the mysticism of DNA and electronics, we ignore that biography is stronger than biology, we neglect the context in which we live and must be evaluated. This abrupt reduction of the body to a size that extols only immediate materiality, whether it be physical or electronic, reduces the very possibility of personal integral knowledge, comprised of complex biological processes, of relations with the environment, relations with other human beings. The body leaves life, and life abandons the body. (Rodotà 2006: 98)

Many rhetorics on prevention nevertheless seem to put the body at their very centre, indeed impose an obsessive attention towards it. Diets, exercise, plastic surgery procedures, preventive and healing cosmetics and diagnostic examinations are constantly exhorted. And yet, nay, because of this, the body seems to lose the role of the place of self in its historical and social, not to mention psychological and carnal 'one-ness', assuming the role of a mere place of ongoing interventions aimed at modifying it, shaping it. This occurs through its decomposition in zones, pieces, fragments, as well as indexes, traces, signs, to the extent where its continuous invention is made possible by the new virtual communication technologies. The imperative is: you can be what you want, and you can become what you want. Aesthetic surgery procedures have even become a television show: it's the myth of Frankenstein in its optimistic version. It's a body confined to and moulded by technique as never before.

Many people welcome the new possibilities for nomadism of identities, the new powers of choice which indeed seem to free us from our bodies: cyborgs and transgenders are celebrated as representing ways to free oneself from pre-established roles in the institution of gender, the technologies of reproduction being read as a way through which one can finally affirm a female freedom that is similar to that of males (see, on this last point, Pitch 1998.)

However, this is precisely the point. The freedom that thus seems to be affirmed is a freedom of choice (today increasingly in terms of consumption of goods) which is inherent to the neutral and abstract individual, with neither body nor sex, a protagonist of modernity. But if, in the first wave of modernity, this individual was strong, and revealed his masculine, adult, proprietary nature, today neutrality and abstractness seem instead to be converted into an incessant possibility of transformation, change, manipulation, fragmentation. It is this fragmentation that is greeted as a possibility for new freedom. Yet it seems to me, on the contrary, that this is not much of an innovation. The freedom that is inherent to the disappearance of the modern individual, or better yet, which is inherent to his fragility, is even more ephemeral and virtual than 'traditional' freedom. While they have multiplied, the choices nevertheless have not changed in substance and quality, but instead unfurl over a universe of ever increasing heteronomous possibilities, which seem to have less and less to do with what actually counts. But we will return to this point later.

The current insistence on individual responsibility therefore extends all the way to the responsibility to choose one's own physical identity, to change it incessantly, to mould one's own body according to imperatives of health and aesthetics that assume the characteristics of true and proper moral imperatives.

Here too, that pressure for independence I talked about can be traced, and its corollary is guilt. If one can be who one wants, one cannot not feel guilty if one is too fat or too thin – ugly according to the dominant aesthetic standards – if we fall ill, if we do or do not have children, if our children, and above all our daughters, are themselves not 'pretty', or healthy in mind and body. Naturally one *cannot* be how one wants, except in virtual reality, and therefore the sense of inadequacy and even guilt is very widespread, while attempts at changing oneself and those close to one are multiplied with every available means.

Therefore, uncertainty and insecurity also, if not above all, invade that sense of self that is tied to one's own corporeity. The imperative to achieve competence turns into a feeling of inadequacy, and interactions with others are marked, even before a mistrust of others, by a mistrust of oneself. From this viewpoint, the body is like the past, it is like that place that some time ago it was easier to leave: the disappearance of the body, like that of the past, makes every departure useless, and every trip and encounter uncertain and fearful.

And yet, as we will see, there are at least two bodies that not only resist but are also perceived, in our societies, as bodies and therefore as being threatening: the female body – and that's a long story – and the migrant's body. Both are connoted by a voracious and aggressive sexuality, which it is necessary to keep at bay and prevent from being exercised. Moreover, the migrant's body is aggressive not only sexually, inasmuch as the possibility of other types of violence is always attributed to it (we will return to the issue of the body as a weapon, as a means for killing, later). Or even: when the bodies are there, they seem dangerous; whoever is perceived as a body is experienced because of this as being dangerous. The danger of these bodies lies precisely in the fact that they are connoted as immutable, weighty, as totally conditioning motivations and choices. The immutability and weightiness of the body is an ingredient not so much of diversity, as we would want it, but of inequality: one is inferior because one is a body – the corporeal being justifies the inequality. The body no longer signifies the future of desire, but the present of pain and death.

Hence the idea of one part of feminism that freedom *from the* body is a requirement for female freedom. But this freedom can only pass through methods and techniques that impose, conversely, a fixation on (parts of) the body itself, and a strenuous discipline that has little to do with freedom. The paradox is that the possibility of choice is based on an intense and growing medicalization of the female body and its functions, and therefore on an accentuated dependency on not only doctors and medicine, but on aesthetic and health standards – one's own and those of any children one might have, – imposed from the outside. Fatima Mernissi (1995) says that size 42 is the burka of Westerners: since the burka is imposed and size 42 is, conversely, a 'free' choice, this statement seems exaggerated. Yet, the Bisturi TV show recently did a live broadcast of a breast augmentation procedure on a twenty-year-old girl.

What is more important, however, is not so much the effort that freeing oneself from the female body seems to entail, the discipline which one must undergo, the norms to which one is subjected, but the fact that this 'liberation' is not at all a prelude to freedom which, as I already said, and I reaffirm here, requires concreteness and corporeity.

The question of political action and the very sense of politics is raised here. Having been left outside the door of (male) politics since the beginning, the current dissolution of the body signals the end of these same politics. Because there was a return to bodies once the care of the *polis* was left behind, and the bodies themselves signified the afterworld of politics it was necessary for politics to be defined as such, i.e., politics: now, the dissolution of bodies announces that a return is impossible, and therefore those politics are in deep crisis.[3]

---

3   Nowadays it is rather common to speak, as far as our Western democracies are concerned, of a shift from representative to representational democracy. Politics is mainly being played out on the media scene, and how one presents oneself is all important.

Today's new politics of new actors justifiably starts instead from the body, and it is in the body that it wants to be situated. I'm talking about the politics ushered in with feminism, which are frankly unimaginable without being situated in the sexual body. Later on we will return to this point as well.

However, returning to prevention, and its current propensity towards the decomposition and dissecting of bodies, not to mention the electronic surveillance systems which render them in vain, this prevention is not only the opposite of politics, but a form of discipline and self-discipline that tries to do without politics, to substitute for it, to make it a useless accessory or pure merchandise, to construe it and present it as at most the professional choice of some. Anti-politics feeds off of many things: one of these things is the generalized imperative of prevention, the discourse on prevention, the disappearance of bodies over which prevention presides.

Mary Douglas (1992), in regard to the domination of the discourse of risk in our cultures, attributes the current depoliticization to the technicality with which are construed choices that in fact are value-laden and therefore political, a technicality that is couched in the vocabulary of probabilities. It is clear that this reading is also valid for prevention, nay, it is most adequate for prevention. But it seems to me that depoliticization is further connected to what I was saying before, that is, to the disappearance of bodies, and that only newly situating ourselves within our bodies can usher in the possibility of politics. Of course, a politics that is different from the kind known up until now, which is currently experiencing a profound crisis, which is also due to the disappearance of bodies.

Pollution

I have said several times how the imperative of prevention assumes moral connotations. I would now like to reflect on another aspect which is connected to this, that is, the notion of pollution (impurity, contamination) which in turn has sacred connotations. Pollution, in anthropology, indicates the contamination of purity, i.e. impurity. Pollution itself is an aspect of the sacred in the sense that contact with the sacred is dangerous. Sanctity and purity both have an ambivalent

---

Charisma comes from being able to act on this scene, and individual charisma seems to be all that counts. Again, we can observe the disappearance of boundaries between public and private and an extreme individualization of politics. The body put on the scene, though, while all-important, is not usually a body one speaks from, a body where one is situated, but rather an actor's mask, to be manipulated at will (the example of our current prime minister is emblematic, but not unique). An exception may be Barack Obama, whose body does tell a complex and complicated story, something of which Obama himself appears to be very well aware.

nature since in both there is the idea of separation: purity, like sanctity, must always be protected (Pasquinelli 2004).

The idea and the metaphor of contamination connote many of the practices and rhetorics of prevention. As in the examples drawn from ancient or traditional populations cited by Mary Douglas (1966), the danger comes from pollution. I'm not referring here so much to the factual occurrence of air pollution or water pollution or food contamination, but rather to the attitude with which this pollution is generally faced, and not only in these glaring cases (see also Beck 1992: 24). It is a semi-religious attitude in which the impure, harmful, poisonous 'substance' is perceived as threatening to health, which is constructed as a moral imperative. The metaphor of pollution extends from air, water and foods to interpersonal relations, through, for example, sexuality. Indeed, 'eating and having sex [in traditional societies] are two functions that are particularly at risk, due to the contact that is established between the inside and the outside' (Pasquinelli 2004: 105).

The way in which the AIDS epidemic has been constructed and perceived, especially at the beginning, is an example of this. It was presented as the ineluctable and deserving outcome of immoral behaviours. And now migrants are often accused of being 'plague spreaders', that is carriers of old and new illnesses, of mysterious germs that could impact upon the physical integrity, not to mention the moral and psychic integrity, of the natives.

In a certain sense, then, many practices of prevention can be viewed as true and proper purification rites, or rites for avoiding impurity. Like these rites in traditional societies, they regulate both behaviours and relations between people, 'guiding all aspects of life' (Pasquinelli 2004: 111). And just as in these societies, it is 'the bodies that are the first to be regimented in a system of exclusion and belonging marked by the pure/impure pair' and '[i]f anyone ever thought that the complex coding of taboos was more restrictive, the work of the modern safety officer should give them pause' (Douglas 1992: 16).

This is an implication, perhaps an unforeseen effect, of many 'green', environmentalist campaigns, especially the most radical ones. In them reappears the idea of 'nature' as a pure, uncontaminated, inherently good place, the preservation of which becomes a task that is not so much – and not just – political but para-religious. The heralded environmental catastrophes assume the connotation of an apocalypse merited by behaviours and attitudes that desanctify nature.

This idea of nature is not new; it dates back to at least the 60s (not to speak of the German *Wandervogel* youth movement of the early 1900s) to the hippie movements, and is now taken up again in New Age theories and practices. Compared to everything that has conversely been corrupted by history and by society, nature is seen as an uncontaminated place, and therefore one of well-being and health. The return to nature, the use of 'natural' substances to cure oneself from or prevent illnesses, the references to nature in the advertising of goods (from the White Mill Italian advert of cereals to many cars) has the sense of a contraposition to science, which is understood as the manipulation, contamination and corruption of nature itself. It is a return which, as in the past, may be couched both in leftist, 'progressive' terms and in radical conservative terms (for example, 'natural' family, 'natural' procreation, etc.), but which is nevertheless a conscious nostalgic about a fantasized secure place.

It is an idea of security that has a lot of mysticism in it, if not religion, and which leads to attributing the disastrous effects of every natural catastrophe to the fault of someone. Earthquakes, volcanic eruptions, floods and droughts refer back to the guilty action of someone or something, guilty insofar as these events, or their effects, were perceived (often rightly, at least as concerns the consequences in losses of human lives) as due to a human activity. Here too, there is a paradox since this attribution of blame is in reality, for us Westerners, made possible by the development of science and technology. It is to the development of science and technology that we attribute this disastrous interference with 'nature'. Yet, at the same time, it is science and technology that we ask to predict and prevent the disasters themselves.

Moreover, nature as the (last) secure place is a paradox in and of itself because for millennia it has been 'nature' and its uncontrollability that have generated insecurity. Today, it is, conversely, the perverse consequences of human attempts to control and dominate 'nature' that come into strong relief, and are what it is we are afraid of: those perverse consequences that assume the characteristic of punishments that are deserved for having dared to defy nature itself, but also, for not knowing how to predict and prevent, through science, these perverse consequences.

Control and Gambling

Prevention attempts to control the future, to determine it, to make it (more) secure. The obsession with prevention seems not to take fate – destiny – into account. If what happens is always someone's fault, then destiny has no role whatsoever. And yet, from financial speculation to the mass dissemination of every possible game of chance, lottery, bet, it seems that, on the contrary, there is both a strong propensity to rely on the future and a feeling that the future does not appear threatening, but rather is limited to the extremely short term. This is one of Ferrarese's (2002) theses which she proves by using as an example financial capitalism's current hegemony over industrial capitalism.

The simplest way to reconcile these two aspects is to say, as seems evident, that they coexist. Or it could even be said that they concern populations that are at least in part different, or at different points in life. However, I believe that the preventive aspect, the aspect of control, is the prevailing one, and that financial speculation and the spread of gambling, while they have the short term as their horizon, are nevertheless not examples of a hypertrophy of the present, but rather of a fear of the more long-term future – a mistrust in the future.

Gambling and lotteries, on the other hand, are not entirely left to chance, but underlined by probabilistic calculations and elaborate computer systems, which reveal an attempt to control luck too. In short, games and lotteries are not examples of a new sense of 'joyous' freedom, but of a 'freedom' that is connoted by insecurity, first of all in one's self.

The decline of strongly normative institutions, which Ferrarese herself talks about – detraditionalization – places the past in default, and along with it 'society', is liberating only to the extent that they burden each person with a weighty individual responsibility with respect to both one's own present and future and that of those close to her. This individual responsibility which is accompanied by the imperative of independence and competence, is simultaneously denied by the proliferation of experts and consultants that are supposed to teach independence – not to mention the fact that the very propensity for gambling may be perceived and construed as a pathology and symptom of dependency, and that when 'common' citizens approach financial speculation and the results, as often happens, are catastrophic, it is these same common citizens that are charged with imprudence, poor competence and culpably risky behaviour.

Risk-taking is a virtue that is urged upon only whoever can afford to do so. Traditionally, by no coincidence, risk-taking is an imperative for adolescent males and youth, while prudence is what's preached to women, imposing the principle of precaution. Gender too is an institution undergoing significant change, but this difference is nevertheless still felt, and at the same time bears witness to the fact that risk-taking is construed as a virtue only for whoever is perceived as strong. Or to put it another way: if, in taking risks, we harm ourselves, this is taken as confirmation of the fact that we should not have taken these risks, that we were not in a position to take them and, therefore, to a large extent, whatever harm we have suffered is our own fault. Taking risks is rational only for whoever can afford it, for whoever has sufficient financial, social and cultural resources to be sheltered from any negative results. For all others, and they are the majority, taking risks is discouraged; it is construed as intrinsically irrational.

And indeed, as Mary Douglas (1992) shows, this is the underlying assumption of risk analysts. Risk, which in reality originally meant a hazard which could have either negative or positive outcomes, is today primarily used as a synonym of danger, even of serious danger. It is mainly with this meaning that Beck (1992) speaks of it and it is with this precise meaning that we talk about a society of risk. In short, the prevailing idea is that taking risks is intrinsically irrational.

The praising of flexibility and precariousness, of continual change, is paradoxically accompanied by a discouragement of risk-taking and an encouragement of risk prevention. Yet both are based, as I already said, on the imperative of do-it-yourself, independence, individual responsibility. As Douglas says (1992: 16): 'Under the banner of risk reduction, a new blaming system has replaced the former combination of moralistic condemning the victim and opportunistic condemning the victim's incompetence.' Hence, I repeat, it is fitting to see prevention as the other side, the complementary side, of risk-taking.

Sennett (2003: 241) says, citing the research of psychologist Daniel Kahnemann, that, for the large majority of today's workers, assuming risks causes depression and anxiety rather than hope: 'people focus more on what they have to lose than to gain; they are being gambled with rather than themselves gambling'. And even, 'at the top, change and risk can thus be managed without a person coming apart. But lower down in the modern institution, risk can be depressing precisely just because these powers are lacking.'

What Fears

Two books, one British, the other American, are both entitled *The Culture of Fear* (Furedi 1997, Glassner 1999). Each includes lists of fears of the societies analysed. In large part, naturally, the fears are the same – crime, migrants, paedophiles, and so on – and are similar to Italian fears. This is not to say the objects considered dangerous should be thought of as 'true' threats, or threats that are worse than other objects and events.

The choice of fears, or in Douglas' words, of the risks to be faced, is a complex affair: we live in a risky, threatening world, full of unforeseen events, but only some are chosen to be prevented. This choice has to do with the prevailing culture, which in turn depends on social organization, on the principles on which the collectivity's organization has been based. What is considered risky is whatever, at a certain time, seems to be threatening to the social order, or is construed as if it were. Furthermore, what is considered threatening is what can be remedied. Namely, it is the solutions, the answers, that construct the problems, rather than vice versa. Furthermore, individual perception of risks has to do with issues similar to what I call the stakes in play, that is, in other words 'the bearing of the particular risk-perceiver's purposes, whether it is seen as integral to them, or peripheral' (Douglas 1992: 46).

For example, in a study on the perception of in/security of men and women in an Italian city of medium size, it was found that both young women and young men declared they had been the subject of unwanted sexual attention. Yet only the young women maintained that they perceived the sexual harassment as threatening; the young men affirmed they had not even paid attention to it, and that they thought the female reactions were excessive, exaggerated. A single event, therefore, is perceived and construed very differently by different individuals. One explanation in this case may be that nothing of true importance was at stake for the young men, while for the young women unwanted sexual attention represented a confirmation that they were physically and psychologically vulnerable to being primarily perceived as objects and sexual prey (Pitch and Ventimiglia 2001).

In any case, the choice of risks has a political, cultural and institutional connotation: there is nothing 'objective' or technical in it. A list of fears will therefore be similar in cultures such as the Italian, British and American cultures of today because they share the same organizational principles, and are to a large degree an analogous culture. However, surely there will be specific fears, typical of particular contexts, groups and subcultures.

It is necessary to consider another aspect. If risks and fears are intrinsically political, this also means they are used for political purposes, essentially to consolidate the existing, or prevailing and dominant social organization. From this point of view, the disciplining effects of practices of prevention and the legitimizing effects of rhetorics of prevention may be read as political ways of reaffirming and supporting the social order:

> Like cash, ready for any type of investment, the capital of fear can be used for any kind of economic or political profit. And so it is. Personal security has become one of the principal, perhaps the principal argument of sales in all types of marketing strategies. 'Law and order', increasingly reduced to the promise of personal safety, has become a major, perhaps the major selling point in political manifestos and electoral campaigns. (Bauman 2005: 70)

In a world in which the risks we run and of which we are more or less aware are not just catastrophic, but dependent on political choices camouflaged by technical needs, and where these choices are increasingly removed, with globalization, from the influence of strong politics at the nation state level, the proliferation of fears and threats towards which, apparently, something can be done conversely assumes the function of maintaining the existing order by shifting demands and requests, not to mention conflicts, onto scapegoats:

> Let us note that – wisely – consumer markets rarely offer cures or preventive medicine against natural dangers, like earthquakes, hurricanes, floods or avalanches; promises of protection and salvation focus as a rule are on dangers

artificially created. The latter have a clear advantage over the former, since they allow fears to be cut to the measure of the available cures, rather than vice versa. (Bauman, 2002: 199)

Analogously, Beck (1992) maintains that today's risk distribution confirms social inequalities. Nay, the risk distribution system has supplanted the resource distribution system in the reproduction of the social order. As previously noted, Beck refers to a reflexive, but all the same quite objectivistic, notion of risks, characterized by those catastrophic risks that are directly connected to the expansion of science and technology. Poverty, says Beck, incurs an unfortunate abundance of risks. While the question of the causes of risks is continuously shifted from one level to another, the responsibility of prevention is in fact displaced onto each one of us, which means that only whoever can support the costs of it and has the necessary informational and knowledge resources can put him or herself – relatively – under shelter.

We will see throughout this text how public policies, and in particular those regarding common crime, use language, rhetorics and practices of prevention that shift the attention from catastrophic risks to risks something can be done about and how, in this way, they reaffirm and establish old and new inequalities. In the next chapter we will take a brief look at issues relating to health, since this is a field where not only, as is obvious, the rhetoric and practices of prevention are particularly widespread and in which it is easy to show the change from a collective and public viewpoint to an individual and private one, but also because they are an important detail of the rhetoric and practices of social control. Indeed, the metaphor of 'immunity', which is of medical origin, can be applied to most discourses regarding prevention, and certainly to those concerning contemporary social control, especially those directed towards protecting 'us' from 'them': 'criminals', migrants, and the whole array of today's outsiders and outcasts.

Chapter 2
Preventing is Better than Curing

Functioning

Preventing, we often say, is better than curing.

Prevention in the field of health has a very ancient history, as Cosmacini reminds us (1994). And the scientific discoveries of the nineteenth and twentieth centuries have glorified the importance and effectiveness of prevention. The prolonging of the average lifespan in wealthy countries and the lowering of infant and maternal mortality rates are among the most evident successes, not so much (or not just) of new cures, but of lifestyles characterized by the prevention of illnesses, the improvement of the economic and social situation, and hence urban renewal and developments in hygiene.

In Italy, the last pandemic due to 'underdevelopment' was perhaps the cholera pandemic in Naples in 1973, which was paradoxically contemporaneous with the illnesses from pollution (that is from 'development') highlighted by the Seveso[1] tragedy in 1976. There was therefore a significant shift from the typical problems of agricultural societies to those of industrialized societies, where the disillusionment that accompanied the latter during their highest phase (the phase preceding decline) was increased by another tragedy, that of thalidomide.[2] The almost unreserved trust that had until then accompanied developments in pharmacology transformed into mistrust, alarm, with respect, on the one hand, to the side effects of all drugs (*pharmakon*, indeed, means both cure and poison), and with respect, on the other, to the pharmaceutical industry, which was suspected of focusing much more on profit than on research geared to the well-being and health of people. Suspicion and mistrust concerning both drugs (and the pharmaceutical industry) and the equally enormous advances made in medical technology henceforth have consistently coexisted with hope and trust in a drug or 'miraculous' technology for resolving all problems.

This contradiction is typical of our time, where it only seems possible to find remedies for the ills of progress with further progress, and so on to infinity, but

---

1   In Seveso, a factory emitted a big cloud of dioxin, which is extremely poisonous and carcinogenic.
2   Thalidomide was a drug prescribed to pregnant women to avoid morning sickness. It caused many babies to be born with deformed limbs.

where this same progress is increasingly experienced with ambivalence, when not openly called into question, through the idea of limit, or even more radically (by feminism) by the critique of its epistemological roots in 'Western' and 'male' science.

In Italy, a social and collective conception of health was affirmed with the 'health movements' connected to the student and worker struggles of 1968 and the following years, but, at the legislative level, it was necessary to wait until 1978, when the health reform was enacted which established the first true national health system. The health struggles had the merit 'of having made not only the working classes, but the entire country, understand the need for prevention, *and therefore for the control and modification of morbigenous environmental conditions*' (Berlinguer 1977: XLVII, emphasis added). This is the conception of prevention that, at least until the 1980s, has prevailed in common sense, if not necessarily in practice.

Prevention was therefore connoted as a public undertaking which must remove, or at least mitigate, both the conditions that facilitate the emergence of pathologies of 'underdevelopment' and, *a fortiori*, those of 'development' (as Berlinguer (1977: 8) said at the time: 'to contrast the genius of healthiness with the evils of underdevelopment and the distortions of progress'), for example accidents at work and the illnesses connected to work in polluting industries. What begins to come forward is 'a more precise attention to the entire metropolitan *quality of life*'. The requirement was set 'that the health awareness that took shape in factories be extended' to all socio-environmental phenomena, in particular to the 'pollution of water and air due to industrial waste and intense private motorization' and to the 'chaos of housing which entails congestion, chaotic traffic and a shortage of green space' (Cosmacini 1994: 191).

The establishment of the national health service, a product of this time period and of this conception, confirmed at the normative level that the issue of health was a public and collective one, and therefore that the responsibility for the risk of becoming ill should be public. Thus, the constitutional norm declaring health a social right, not an individual duty, was finally implemented.

This is not to say that, at the level of actual policies, things really went this way, but it is important to emphasize the prevailing political rhetoric, as well as the corresponding widespread common sense. Health and illness obtained the status of a public issue, and it was a public responsibility and duty to act on the causes of morbidity which were viewed as being primarily social and environmental, as well as a duty of collective solidarity to insure, by passing from individual contribution to the general taxation system, everyone against the risk of becoming ill.

With the Workers' Statute (1970) '[t]he right to health was transformed into an element that was no longer supplementary, but fundamental, intrinsic to the work relationship and demanding the preliminary respect of the employer' (Cosmacini 1994: 78). Prevention was the cornerstone of the new discourse on health and illness, not to mention of the discourse on medicine and its duties, which took place among 'democratic' health workers in the decade between 1968 and 1978 (1978 being the year when the law instituting the national health service was enacted). It was a type of prevention that was conceived as a collective taking charge of every type of risk connected to life in advanced industrial societies, and which availed itself of epidemiological research aimed at finding out not only the biological causes, but also, and especially, the social and economic causes of hardships and illnesses that had gone from acute to chronic.

How distant this conception of prevention was from the one prevailing today is made clear by the words of Maccacaro (1972: XXXV), who put it this way as early as in 1972:

> another of today's myths is 'the early diagnosis': this predictive medicine, exchanged for preventative medicine, has nothing to do with a medicine that aims to find out the causes of pathologies in the living and work environment, and therefore turns out to be totally inadequate except for the purpose of generating a false sense of security.

But in reality this is precisely what is happening today: the early diagnosis, which has become even more developed and effective than when Maccacaro was writing, is presented as the principal method for preventing the risks of significant illnesses and, furthermore, is prescribed in the current discourse as a practice that each and every one of us must individually, and necessarily privately (given the waiting times in public organizations), carry out. The attention to primary prevention, as is called prevention that is targeted at intervening in the causes of illnesses – social, environmental, as well as lifestyle – in the context of medicine and health policies, and which was several times affirmed as decisive until the 1980s, is in fact very rare and is becoming even rarer with the development and invention of technologies and drugs that are instead aimed at 'secondary' prevention, namely early diagnoses and therapies.

In health circles, the conflict between epidemiologists, who are interested in primary prevention, and clinicians and scientists, who orient themselves towards secondary prevention, seems to have been won by the latter. For example, it is known and said that at least 90 per cent of cancers are caused by environmental factors – pollution, food poisoning and so on – so much so that the incidence of deaths from cancer is not only not decreasing, but appears to be rising. And yet, the funds dedicated to epidemiological research are just one meagre part of the amount dedicated to clinical and molecular biology (Cosmacini 1994).

Prevention is, by nature, egalitarian and universalistic, that is, capable in theory of providing protection to all strata of the population against the risk of falling ill, while secondary prevention is only accessible to those who can afford it in terms of financial resources, but also social and cultural ones.

The erosion of social rights, and among them the all-important right to health, implies that the advances of preventive diagnostics are not within every man and woman's reach. As medical technological instruments and advances in genetics seem to increasingly promise prevention not only against illnesses – the so-called pathologies – but against old age itself, and life as a whole is medicalized (in order to get to a future in which life should last, as a rule, up to 120 years), their use becomes more difficult, often impossible, for large segments of the population. These various progresses, and the ideology supporting and deriving from them, produce anxiety, concern and feelings of guilt; if one must be 'healthy' (we'll see later what this term means today), if the means for diagnosing future pathologies are known to exist, but these means are not accessible, one does not live better, but less well.

On the other hand, major investments in the biomedical sciences, above all in diagnostics and genetics, denote a trend towards parenthesizing the social, collective and even psychological 'causes' of illnesses so as to reduce them to phenomena that are caused by malfunctions of strictly biological elements. At the same time, the area that is considered pathological and in need of medical or pharmacological intervention comes to be expanded.

Some have talked about there being a hegemony of surveillance medicine over hospital medicine, dating as far back as the start of the last century when the chain of symptom, sign and illness was entirely reorganized. In hospital medicine, the symptom referred to the (concrete) sign and this referred back to the 'illness'. Surveillance medicine reorganizes the chain horizontally, with symptom, sign and illness all becoming factors that predict risk. In fact, symptoms today may not be there at all since in being entrusted to surveillance medicine the body gives way to an extracorporeal space that is often identified with 'lifestyle'.

Whereas the meaning of prevention changes, in the sense that preventing now tends to mean not so much taking care of the social and environmental causes of many pathologies, but refining the instruments of early diagnosis so that each individual can (and must) take care of themselves (in addition to the prescription of a countless series of behaviours and attitudes that assail one's lifestyle as a whole and the minutest choices of daily life), 'curing' also changes meaning. 'Curing' means less and less to go to the roots of the pathology or disorder and more and more to enable people to 'function' *despite* pathologies or disorders.

'Functioning', in turn, does not simply mean learning to live with pathologies or disorders that cannot be cured, but being efficient, independent, autonomous. With respect to the category of the 'pathological', the category of 'functioning' lends itself to an even broader and more extensive application. We know that the normal/pathological pair is a pair that is strongly connoted by the viewpoint of prevailing cultural models and values, but the functional/dysfunctional pair, apparently more 'technical' and less evaluative, is in reality even more strictly oriented towards extra-biological principles and criteria of efficiency and individual responsibility.

The biomedical knowledge of the nineteenth century, and the life sciences in general, 'problematized bodily and populational life into a series of highly publicized risks and crises' (Katz and Marshall 2004: 54). Therefore, the normal/pathological pair used for this purpose today seems to have been replaced, or even accompanied by, the functional/dysfunctional pair where *enablement* is the standard. This standard is a bio-cultural standard, in the sense that it incorporates mixed criteria, insofar as the boundaries between 'nature' and 'culture' have become confused, fluid, permeable.

The real and the artificial, the human and the non-human, merge and there are forms of life that are simultaneously both things or neither of the two. The notion of functionality at once includes nature and artifice, technology, culture, and has the advantage of being fit for a measurability that is based on the bio-cultural standard of enablement. The objective of this standard is 'doing', not 'being' – 'doing' in the sense of being able to function without help, without depending on some program or service. This means that one can certainly have 'pathological' problems, but what counts is if, how and the extent to which appropriate pharmacological cures or instruments succeed in enabling one to adequately 'function' (that is, without help) despite these pathologies.

The philosophy of functionality and enablement are in many ways analogous to the administrative and managerial ideologies that we will observe in the field of strategies and policies of social control where the aim is not to address the 'causes' of crime and hardship, but instead to act so as to minimize the problems that these phenomena cause for the citizenry. Here too, what counts is enabling people to best function, namely without dependence on programs, services and so on, rather than facing the 'causes' of the pathologies.

The harm reduction strategies applied to drug addiction, for example, can be interpreted in this way. They have two explicit objectives: protecting non-addicts from thefts and pickpocketing aimed at getting money for drugs, and simultaneously working so that the addicts themselves can 'function' without having to give up drugs.

Moreover, this example shows how the do-it-yourself ideology of autonomy and independence can support completely different strategies, since the therapeutic community, to which harm reduction is supposed to be an alternative, but which conversely relies on 'freedom' from drugs, also has as its objective the reconstruction of the personality of the addict around the principles of autonomy, independence and individual responsibility. There are many different types of therapeutic communities. But most of them appear to work with behavioural techniques where the search for the addict's past history and motivations is underplayed.

This example also shows how 'managerial' policies, both in the field of social control and in that of health (which are after all often intertwined), may often themselves be informed by and simultaneously propagate ethical principles and values.

'Functioning' may actually be in many cases a better choice than 'curing'. A similar type of philosophy was part of the inspiration for our psychiatric reform, initiated with the deinstitutionalization of the inmates of Gorizia psychiatric hospital at the end of the 1960s and which finally become law in 1978. The idea was (and is, in those psychiatric services which still work in this manner) to help those suffering from a psychiatric handicap to live a 'normal' life, outside of closed institutions, through a complex series of measures: drugs, of course, and psychotherapy when appropriate, but also protected housing, jobs, etc.; that is, 'curing' may not mean the disappearance of the illness or of its symptoms when this is impossible, but 'enabling' the patient to cohabit with her handicap as best as possible.

Independence and autonomy are very good things, especially when the alternative is institutionalization or some other type of exclusion from social life. Independence and autonomy may turn into problems, though, if in order to reach them the search for 'deeper' causes is abandoned or massive recourse to symptomatic drugs is the only adopted measure.

Sexuality and sterility are other examples of biomedical interventions geared towards 'functioning' rather than towards removing the causes of possible pathologies. Sexuality is first reduced to heterosexual penetration, and secondly to male erectile dysfunction (however, this model is also used for 'treatments' of female orgasm difficulties); and then male erectile dysfunction is no longer questioned at the biological level, and even less so at the psychological or relational level, but is instead 'resolved' through drugs like Viagra. The sales data for these drugs indeed show how widely they are used: well above the levels of assessed and prolonged conditions of impotence due to organic factors. Here, the philosophy of 'functioning', where functioning is equivalent to being able to practice sexuality, understood as penetration, produces a widespread pressure on individuals, who are induced to use drugs in order to always be 'efficient'.

The question of AIDS has caused sexuality in general to be reconstructed as 'risky'. HIV tests on the one hand construct specific at-risk categories (homosexuals, addicts, prostitutes), and on the other hand are suggested to everybody (there are studies that show how a large majority of heterosexuals are now willing to take the test). And AIDS is an opportunity for extensive campaigns of prevention which, in addition to recommending abstinence, also recommend caution, attention and the use of condoms.

As for sterility, now the research seems to be concentrating on assisted procreation techniques which do not treat sterility in and of itself, but circumvent it; that is, they attempt to enable people to procreate even though they are sterile. Here too, 'adequate' functioning is more important than the treatment of a pathological or 'abnormal' condition. What counts is efficiency, understood as the capacity to perform.[3]

Psychical disorders is another field where research on causes has now been abandoned, or at least reduced to dysfunctions at the biochemical level, here too excluding any psychological and relational problems. First of all, the definition of disorder or illness in the psychological field is becoming wider: as I already noted, even bad moods fall within this category now since bad moods and sadness are 'dysfunctional' in the sense that they do not permit complete efficiency. There is a magic pill for everything: for children's inattention at school, and for more or less serious states of depression. The question is no longer, what do symptoms mean, but, how can we eliminate their dysfunctional effects?[4]

The imperative to be healthy is transformed into an imperative to be functional, that is, efficient, independent, and therefore to do whatever possible to prevent the condition of dependency. It is not so much pathology that must be prevented, but dysfunctionality.

And what is more dysfunctional than living out one's old age in poor health, dependent on social assistance or the help of family members? Old age is increasingly treated as an illness that can, and therefore must, be prevented. The entire course of life, being what leads to old age, is transformed into a series of problems and conditions that must be treated and, even before that, prevented, in order to arrive at a responsibly functional old age.

---

3   By this, there is no intention to stigmatize these techniques or whoever asks to make use of them. The only intention is to bring to light the type of medical culture they imply, and which these techniques contribute to producing.

4   But the question lies not only in the inattention to individual intra-psychical problems and motivations. More essentially, it is the social conditions behind many individual illnesses that are completely neglected, not questioned, not discussed: see, here too, Benasayag and Schmit 2004.

Just as in the case of social control policies, as we shall see, the individual and collective conditions of social and economic hardship impede access to the goods and resources that are necessary for a 'healthy' life, and, therefore, an 'efficient' old age. In the heart of the West, in the US, where these medicalization processes are stronger and more evident, and where not even the germ of a public health service exists, the life expectancy of the poorest segments of the population *is decreasing*, just as the mortality rate in the first year of life is increasing.[5]

It is above all the question of health that is at the centre of so-called welfare reforms (along with education and social security) in most of Europe. Cuts in public spending, a trend towards a 'cut and dry' bureaucracy, partnerships, outsourcing, delegations to the private and private-social sectors end up penalizing the 'less privileged' who are the recipients of inferior services and insufficient treatments, just when the state's responsibility for taking care of what produces illness and morbidity in the living and work environments is decreasing.

I said that the body tends to disappear, dissected into thousands of increasingly tiny pieces, each one of them subjected to the attention of various experts. The combination of the expansion of the area of pathology and the ever growing sectorization of both the body and knowledge of it, along with the development of diagnostics and the reduction of public financing for health, produce a paradoxical situation which is very difficult to face for individuals who are constantly urged to take care of themselves.

The prevalence of a 'functioning' trend in the medical clinical context, whatever its merits, testifies to a 'flattening' of our social and cultural scenario. By this I mean the loss of the third dimension – depth, verticality. The irrelevance of the past, the crisis of classical 'vertical' institutions such as political parties, the 'flattening' of the organization of production and bureaucracies, and finally the domination of 'functioning' over the search for deeper causes, all point to the prevalence of the horizontal dimension in our time.

Mad Cows and Other Strange Animals

Recently we have all been subjected to a few great scares that have to do with diseases variously associated with animals: mad cow disease, bird flu (H1N1) and swine flu. Fortunately, only relatively few people have contracted these diseases and even fewer have died (in the West). But for days, weeks, even months the mass media, the WHO (World Health Organization), innumerable medical doctors and

---

5   All over the West, poorer people are fat, better off people are slim. The pressure to be fit contrasts with the pressure to consume – especially junk food. But junk food is tasty and, what's more important, cheap.

not a few politicians have been involved in scaring all of us about the imminent spread of pandemics potentially as dangerous as the Spanish flu of the early 1900s, and all the more threatening because of globalization.

I am not interested here in discussing either the reasons or the consequences of these periodic scares: I just want to stress how they are connected to the sense of guilt we have internalized – perhaps rightly so – towards the way we have been interfering with 'nature'. These illnesses are presented as nature rebelling and avenging itself upon us, the rich of the world. Yet, what we are insistently required to do is not so much to amend our ways (actually, the ways in which the big corporations are abusing agriculture) but to take personal measures not to become ill ourselves, by avoiding eating beef, by going around masked, by refraining from travelling to 'risky' places, all of which are pitiful measures in our times of course, but enough, if not to reassure, to put back the onus of safety upon each of us.

Again, personal prevention is privatized and couched in moral terms, both because we all feel somewhat guilty for these diseases, and because we are made responsible for avoiding them.

Genetics, Diagnoses, Prediction

The development of genetic research seems to rely not on 'functioning', but on addressing the very root of the 'causes' of poor functioning through intervention in defective genes. What combines the two trends, at least in part, is the parenthesizing of the cultural and social environment as not only the possible 'causes' of problems, but also as those which can contribute to making them less serious, less discrimination producing, less onerous for people.

The extreme biological reductionism that cloaks the ideologies justifying genetic research, in particular the Genome Project, seems to bring us back to the first modernity, the 'solid' modernity, wherein all problems, not just biological, but social and economic problems as well, are traced to the malfunctioning of genes, to defective genes. This results not only in an ideology, but in a true and proper utopia: the utopia of a 'perfect health', not only human health, but that of the world, not only physical health, but psychical and social health.

It appears as if, once again, scientific reason, in the more technical and reductive sense of the term, seeks to control human and non-human nature in order to produce a bright future. Thus it would seem that the idea of a complete control of the future through scientific undertaking, in this case genetic research, has made a triumphant return.

Presented as the way to find the Holy Grail, in other words to reveal not only and not so much the origins of both physical and psychical illnesses and pathologies, but the ultimate secrets of human beings, genetic research and in particular the Genome Project bring us to an ideology that was typical of 'solid' modernity, that is, the promise of a solution to all human problems, even social and economic ones, through the manipulation and elimination of their primary causes, today to be discovered in some gene defect. Here, prevention truly means firmly anchoring the future not so much to the present, but to the correction of a biological 'past' – our own genes. The predetermination of a human, but also environmental, future through the manipulation of what is presented as the origin of all problems (including 'deviance', the problem of homelessness, armed conflicts) refers back to the utopias and scientific ideologies of the 1800s, and revives the bet on 'progress' guided by reason and science.

> Genetic testing and genetic screening are presented as multifunctional, and therefore their use is urged in the most diverse sectors: from prevention and treatment of illnesses to the fight against crime, from personal identification to the entering of employment and insurance contracts, and so on. The general effects of this trend, independently of their positive or negative evaluation, can be summarized by speaking about individualization, classification, control. (Rodotà 2006: 178)

Naturally, all this is not the 'fault' of the developments and successes of molecular biology and genetics over these last 30 years. The point is that these developments come to be viewed through the lenses of a cultural and political climate, as I have said many times, the characteristics of which are the pre-eminence of the individual and the crisis of ideas, not to mention the practices, relating to a collective, and therefore public, responsibility over what can happen to the individual. This is not to say that scientific research is entirely innocent, both because it benefits from more financing when it is directed towards objectives that are dear to the dominant elites, which are after all the ones who pay, and because many scientists not only seem to share, but do their best to provide, data that support reductionist and determinist arguments.

What some science indeed says is that the environment, in and of itself, does not count, that social and economic affairs don't count, but what is truly important and what we must concentrate on is defective-gene intervention. Much of this rhetoric is expanded, magnified and distorted by the media, but the fact remains that, unlike the recent past, the research is focused on the biological rather than the social 'causes' of ills and problems. Perhaps there is so much mistrust of the possibilities of intervening in social causes through politics that the promise of the most reductionist biological science tends to be favourably received.

Nevertheless, this favourable reception is thick with perplexity and mistrust, as the crusade against genetically modified foods demonstrates. Indeed these foods are widely perceived as bearers of risk, although it is not entirely clear what risk, that is whether it is biological or economic (in relation to the traditional agricultures of the world's South, for example). Genetically modified foods have in fact been around for a long time, the novelty being only (but this is no small thing, naturally) that now the modification occurs by grafting genes taken from organisms that are different than those into which they are inserted (Lewontin 2001). We could then understand both the promotion and the success of this crusade to be based on a reasonable principle of precaution and prudence, but in reality this crusade often assumes apocalyptic tones and connotations, as if all of the mistrust and lack of confidence in regard to science and technology that have been building up over the last 30 years were being unloaded onto these foods.

However, the bigger problems relating to genetic research, and its current predominance, with respect to both other types of scientific research and their echo in the mass media, as well as the ideology that they promote, are due to the split between advances in diagnostics and the relative stasis of therapy. Many hereditary illnesses are now predictable through genetic testing, and DNA zones have been found for others where one or more 'defective' genes are probably located, but there are (still) no cures for many of these illnesses.

And there is another fundamental consideration to be made: even illnesses correlated to mutations, or at least some of them (for example, haemophilia), can develop and be managed very differently according to how and how many health and social resources are made available to confront them. That's not all: what is found in the genotype will not necessarily be found in the phenotype. A mutation may raise, in the population, the risk of developing a certain pathology, and yet this does not mean that many of the carriers of the mutation itself will develop it. Here too, the influence of environmental factors can be decisive.

Predictability creates many problems due to the fact that while it is obviously expressed in probabilistic terms of risk, in many cases there is not much to be done once one finds out that he is a bearer of the malformation linked to the illness.

There is not much to be done for individuals, but this information may be very important for private insurers, employers and, not least of all, the public health system. Examples are not lacking: let's consider, for example, the requests for genetic testing by private insurers and employers. With respect to the risk of getting sick, when the probability is very high, and there are no cures, it is not the individual who benefits from this knowledge, even if some studies have shown that bearers of the Huntington chorea gene, who are certainly destined to get sick, preferred to know that they carry the gene. It is where there are no laws that prohibit it, that the employers and, above all, the insurance companies draw the major benefits from genetic testing (Rodotà 2006).

We then often find ourselves faced with tragic choices, for example when one is the bearer of a mutation responsible for a certain type of breast cancer. Here, the choice is between removing both breasts, which is a significant mutilation for a woman, or taking the risk of getting sick.

But sometimes, or often, it is not a matter of true and proper opportunities for individual choice, however tragic. Debating the differences between applying eugenics to populations, as the Nazis did, and the eugenics practised by the social democracies of Northern Europe until the 1960s, and the choices that individuals today can make through diagnoses on pre-implanted embryos, Harris (1992) notes that the latter eugenics do not appear, initially, as a eugenics of populations as they are dependent on the choices of individuals. And yet, these choices may already be, or become in the very near future, practically obligatory; for example, when the risk of having a handicapped baby is strongly discouraged by the attitude of private insurers, and by the pressures of a national health service, where it exists, which increasingly less frequently takes care of disorders and pathologies. Or even, and more probably, when cultural pressure towards 'normalcy' is very strong, and not only are economic and social resources not provided to confront the problem, but this problem is the source of stigmatization and discrimination.

Thus these are tragic choices, also because in many cases the pre-implantation diagnosis is a probabilistic diagnosis, not only with respect to the risk of the embryo developing the illness, but also with respect to the degree of severity of the illness itself. Plus the fact that, as noted, it is the conditions of the social environment that in many cases determine whether a certain pathology will or will not be incapacitating. In short, when the burden of assuming responsibility for problems becomes individual and private, the pressure to prevent them at any cost, including discarding embryos that are at risk of developing some illness, can become very strong. Thus, the decline of institutions as well as of ideologies of social solidarity, along with the advances of predictive medicine, can push towards the direction of a eugenics that is not so different from one that was geared towards 'improving the race'.

The intertwined questions of what is meant by 'normality' and how much it is valued and how 'equality' is produced are relevant here. Normality is a historical and cultural concept, which is often accompanied by the stigma, discrimination and exclusion of whoever is defined or perceived as 'not normal'. The history of mental illness is too well known to take it up again here. This history exemplifies the changes in how we define mental illness, as well as how the ways used to reckon with it vary through time and space.[6] Nevertheless, nowadays we are in the presence of scientific and technological innovations that may render the pressure to be normal even more restrictive, simultaneously creating a 'caste society' (Rodotà 2006) where the conditions for a true welcoming of the 'otherwise able' and an effective and universal right to health are lacking.

> Definitively, the acceptance of handicaps, whether genetic or of another nature, does not imply a general dissemination of a 'culture of life' that individuals are left to confront alone. The bigger the social acceptance, the bigger the individual acceptance. Without the assumption of social responsibility, placing the accent on individual responsibility can end up abandoning individuals when they face tragic choices.[7] (Rodotà 2006: 173)

I would add that this also involves continuously dismantling the dominant conception of normality, producing and supporting culturally, economically and socially different visions, different ways of living and 'being – fully – human'.

The development of predictive medicine and prevention imply one another, as is clear. They can lead to incredible successes, as in the case of the near eradication of thalassaemia in Sardinia. But they also open up disturbing scenarios, precisely because predictive medicine locates one's own destiny in the discovery of defects in one's individual genetic patrimony. The much acclaimed, but unfounded, attempts at finding the 'schizophrenia gene' or the gene for homosexuality, of locating in the genetic patrimony the causes of social problems like alcoholism, drug addiction and crime can legitimize the abandonment of strategies and policies of social and collective intervention and lead to methods of 'prevention' that are discriminatory and exclusionary, when not worse.

The dream of total prevention through genetic manipulation is rather a nightmare. It is a nightmare that is closely linked to setting apart the social and cultural factors that contribute to making us the people we are, the weight of the economic and political inequalities in determining what we may become, and lastly the social resources we are able to use to live better.

---

6   There was a great slogan from the Olinda association, which for some years worked in the former Paolo Pini psychiatric hospital in Milan which said: 'Up close no one is normal.'

7   The issue is not prohibiting the diagnosis of the pre-implanted embryo in the name of the 'culture of life', as was done in Italy with Law 40 on assisted procreation. On the contrary, it concerns, first of all, the guarantee of the right to health of women and their freedom, as well as making social, economic and cultural resources available in support of people who are born, or who become, as we say today, 'otherwise-abled'.

The current cultural climate promotes and facilitates simplification, concealment and disinterest in the analysis of the influence of social factors, and thus weakens the implementation of methods of prevention that are social. Diseases are traced back to an individual origin, to be found in one's own genetic patrimony or in one's own lifestyle; it is therefore the responsibility of individuals to face them: the collectivity is exonerated from any responsibility whatsoever:

> Imagining that our genes determine us can at times lead to a de-responsibilizing role … And this is in full accord, at the social level, with individualism and with the refusal of solidarity, using precisely the logic of a capitalistic country, agreeing with the refusal of the other and with the affirmation of the irremediable nature of differences. (Jordan 2002: 136)

More On Bodies

I return here to the question of bodies, which is indeed the issue linking the various methods of social control inspired by prevention, and in particular linking those methods legitimized by the call to health and those legitimized, as we will see, by the call to safety and security, in their meaning of a decrease in the risk of becoming a victim of a crime.

Bodies are perceived as a threat: peoples' own bodies, insofar as they are places that hide and host bacteria, germs, defective genes, or tend to assert themselves with their unpleasant characteristics, 'excess' fat, flabby muscles, wrinkles, baldness, odours, secretions, *impurities*. Those of others, when they occupy the spaces we consider to be our own, and especially when their odours, postures, gestures, ways of moving, dressing, and, in short, of living, are different than those we recognize as being 'normal'.

As previously alluded to, there are above all two threatening bodies: the bodies of women and the bodies of migrants. About these bodies, it can be said that the ones that remain in their entirety, in their weightiness, inevitable and impossible to get rid of, are those marked by 'difference' or, conversely, those that we want to mark as 'different'. It is precisely because they are bodies that they are threatening, and if they are threatening they are to be avoided, segregated, regulated and the threats they carry with them prevented.

Modernity, as Foucault says (1975), emerges through a strong and rigorous disciplining of bodies, a discipline that becomes self-discipline and which takes the form of individual freedom, of the construction of the individual's subjectivity. Extreme modernity, the modernity in which we live, tends to dissolve bodies as the very consequence of their intense disciplining, through a labour of dissection, division into smaller and smaller pieces of organs and functions, so that they may be adapted to a machine, right down to the current interchangeability and that mixture of biology and technology that results in the so-called post-human body.

Naturally, women's bodies have also undergone discipline, but the control they have been subjected to is not so much (or mostly) impersonal, as that to which male bodies are subjected. Rather, it is quite personal because it is managed by men themselves, to the extent that women's subjectivity as individuals, the freedom recognized to men, is not, as has been said, within their reach. It is because they have remained bodies to men that they are bodies even now, threatening then and even more threatening today when women themselves demand control over them. The female body is the nature over which (male) culture had to exercise its domination. In this sense, insofar as it is more 'natural' than male bodies, the female body did not dissolve as a consequence of modernity, but remains, weighty, marking women as unequal.

But it is possible to look at the other side of the coin, as women, and not only they, did in the 1960s and 1970s: the 'deviance' from this discipline, the excess attributed to women because of a body that in part escapes impersonal discipline, can become a place of resistance and a driving force for criticism of the existent. Yet, this becomes possible only through a reconquering of the body that does not reassimilate it to 'nature' or dissolve it entirely in language, temptations that are both present in feminist thought and practices.

Meanwhile, this body remains a body and therefore remains a threat and a danger, even to women themselves. It is no coincidence that the female body is more medicalized than the male body, the practices of prevention more precise and extensive, and the self-vigilance that this requires more intense.

As for inequality, it is not so much produced by one being seen as being in possession of a body, but rather the opposite: those who are subordinated and marginalized are viewed as bodies, and almost exclusively as such, or are reduced to them. The migrants, vagrants, addicts, the mentally ill, the homeless of our cities all appear as the main figures of urban insecurity and fear in the various surveys, and they appear as such, it can be maintained, because they are 'corporealized', visible as bodies without further mediations, connoted by all that is reduced and regulated in 'normal' life: filth, disorder, odours. And what causes fear is locked away and segregated; therefore inmates too are above all threatening bodies, just as being labelled a 'criminal' precedes becoming a prison inmate.

Male and female migrants are first and foremost bodies because they are viewed as such because of the differences in attitudes, dress, skin colour and odours that characterize them. If they are male, their body is doubly threatening, connoted by violence (migrants are 'criminals') and hypersexuality (migrants are 'rapists'). If they are female, they participate in the threat of all females, sexuality, as well as, insofar as they are foreign, a sexuality that is even more disruptive (they are prostitutes). And both have dangerous bodies because they are sources of contagion, bearers of mysterious and devastating illnesses.

It is no coincidence that the major intolerances on the part of natives emerge when male and female migrants leave houses, factories and workplaces and gather and meet at some location in the city, such as in front of a station, on the grounds around a church. They talk, and we don't understand what they are saying. It seems to us that their voices are too loud, their gestures and behaviours too emphatic, the food they cook too perfumed. They make a mess, cause filth and disorder. In a word, they are invaders: they invade urban space, at that point already perhaps deserted because we are elsewhere, in the virtual squares of the Internet or in the secure and surveilled major shopping centres, those urban spaces that we lay claim to as our own, marked by our symbols, our practices, our experiences, and which now appear to us as contaminated, 'impure', part of an 'impurity' that concerns bodies that are too corporeal.

In cities, ethnic spatialization certainly has much to do with, first of all, the housing market, male and female migrants densely gathering where it costs less and grouping themselves in more or less homogenous communities as a result of the tendency to join those who arrived before them. Yet this can assume aspects of violent restriction, when native or neighbouring residents impose, sometimes by force, segregation, separation, distance, all of which can be read as attempts at stabilizing and controlling a changing environment, at producing something predictable (Body-Gendrot and Duprez 2001), as well as at sterilizing one's 'own' territory from bodies that are the bearers of threatening diversity.

This is, perhaps, one of the nexuses between difference and inequality. Those who are different (from us) are 'impure' – or alternately, nowadays, have very visible bodies that are construed as if they possessed and determined the people that 'have' them, which, in and of itself, means to be impure since today all of our energy seems to go into attempting to free ourselves from our bodies and from the signs of corporeity (odours, etc.).

This is not in contradiction to the almost obsessive attention that one is asked to dedicate to one's own body, because much of this attention seems precisely directed at eliminating what makes people 'different': illnesses, handicaps, physical marks that are not in keeping with the aesthetic norm. At the same time, those who intentionally mark their own body, with tattoos, piercings, exaggerated makeup, want to make themselves visible and defy the shared norms. However, in reality they too obey the imperative to treat one's own body as subjugated matter, demonstrating that one can do with it what one wants. Extreme interventions in one's own physicality, like Michael Jackson's innumerable plastic surgery operations or those of the artist Orlane, certainly display the body, but not as something that one 'is', but rather as something that one possesses in order to do what one wants with it. This has nothing to do with the determinism attributed to women, migrants, and all of the others that are so-called 'different'. It is both a biological and a cultural determinism, or even the biological and the cultural are viewed as closely implicating one another: the notion of ethnicity, a term which is by no coincidence only used for non-natives, that is non-whites and replaces the now unpronounceable (although not by the uneducated or members of the *Lega* – a xenophobic Italian party, part of the present government coalition) notion of race, but much of it remains, indeed almost all of it. Ethnicity, in fact, both in the common meaning and in the public discourse, refers back to a naturalization of traditions and cultural models which leads to considering foreign bodies as contaminated and dangerous in and of themselves, in that at the same time they are seen as bearers of biological illnesses and of social and cultural deviance.

The female body is first of all 'heavy' for women themselves. In many so-called primitive societies menstruating women are isolated and must engage in particular behaviours in order to not contaminate food, objects, people. And indeed, veils, burkas and similar garments can also be seen, and are indeed justified, as ways of preventing the unleashing of male sexual drives and, therefore, possible male acts of violence. In our societies this takes the form of women practising prudent female behaviours and attitudes when living in the city, whereas their abandonment of these attitudes, if they suffer some act of aggression, backfires against them.

It is, however, true that the female body is, in our society, exhibited, put on display, used to sell merchandise of all kinds, being itself merchandise, at the same time as a widespread rhetoric preaches chastity as the method of preventing physical, moral and social illnesses. It is as if there were no longer anything between chastity and indecency.[8] This insistent display of the body, which is for the most part serial, in other words similar to any other female body, strictly deprived of expressivity and singularity, separate from the person who 'possesses' it, affirms its status as object but, paradoxically, separates it from carnality, sensuality, 'naturality', instead offering it up as a virtual fetish. It is the pre-eminence of seeing, of sight, over every other sense. It is another, less obvious, way of 'sterilizing' female bodies, of depriving them of danger and threat – for men, since for women this denaturalization legitimizes violence and abuse against them. The extensive literature on pornography, both the graphic and visual kind, and its use, even on the Internet, hints at this. It is the contact with real women, carnal, sexual and sensual contact with women in flesh and bone, bodies and minds, that is threatening, risky, to be avoided, and all the more so given that today women are everywhere, no longer hidden within the walls of a house, but present in places of work, study, in squares and in streets.

---

8   This observation is owed to Ida Dominijanni.

It is no coincidence that not only are true and proper laws multiplying, but also codes for internal use in workplaces and universities. The laws and codes punish sexual blackmail and harassment with the aim of preventing aggression against people who are yet again reduced to object-bodies, whereas women 'incarnate' cause fear (and women themselves are asked to wear clothes that neutralize the dangerous weight of their bodies – in short, to dress up as men if they don't just want to avoid harassment but actually want 'to be taken seriously'). These codes, rather than being in defence of women, are in reality defensive devices for men, both because they shield men from possible accusations and because they place a secure distance between the sexes and sterilize the places of work and study from the danger of sexuality.

But there are other ways to 'conceal a perturbing body'. 'The purpose of the research and experimentation on ectogenesis, e.g. on gestation outside the female body, is precisely to exclude the need for that body, and leads to talk of a "superfluous mother"' (Rodotà 2006: 97).

Contact, contagion: the sterilization of bodies and environments proceeds hand in hand with discipline, selection, labelling, all the way to degradation and that definitive sterilization, death. As we will see, preventive war avails itself of the same devices, either to justify itself or through actual practices, only one aspect of which is torture.

Difference is first inscribed on bodies themselves, when it is not immediately visible, and then fixed in biological eternity or in the eternity of a biologized 'culture' through recourse to the category of ethnicity, a more prudish term than race, and then ultimately annihilated insofar as difference is contagious and contaminating. Ethnic cleansing repeats the *Shoah*, and this in turn brings modernity's practices of selection, labelling and stigmatization to the extreme. In these practices, and in their justification, it is not only nation states that are implicated, or the 'ethnic groups' that aspire to become nation states, but also single individuals, each and everyone of us, as we follow the internalized imperative of taking care of oneself and keeping a distance from diversity. This occurs together with, not at all paradoxically, the multiplication of differences themselves, even their demand and invention, which are moves that separate by distinguishing, by trying to impose limits and boundaries on what conversely risks being confused.

The multiplication of differences and keeping a distance from the differences thus reconstructed implicate one another. This is a worrisome affair, especially when keeping distance seems to no longer be sufficient and 'cleansing' is the next resort. The positioning of boundaries between different 'ethnic communities' in cities, already a practice that is not innocent, as we will see in the next chapter on social control, can become the first step in a segregation that is a prelude to 'cleansing'.

Prevention and security therefore produce, or may produce given the necessary circumstances, a stigmatization that uses bodies and is inscribed on them, on those bodies that are presented as such or are experienced and reconstructed as irreducible to sterilization and therefore threatening, bearers of contagion and disorder, and which must be repelled, segregated, and lastly, ultimately, annihilated.

One hypothesis which is in part similar we find in Appadurai (2005) who, in the context of interpreting the brutal violence against 'ethnic minorities', refers to Mary Douglas, demonstrating a symbolic-structural link 'between categorical mixture, the cognitive anguish this incites, and the consequential aversion to spurious taxonomies that is manifested in all moral and social universes' (ibid. 45). The body serves as a symbolic map, and in it are amassed 'vast cosmological conceptions of social categories and classifications' (ibid. 73). However, according to Appadurai, cosmologies today are not 'given', but are instead continuously evolving, and this requires the logic of categorical mixture and of the danger identified by Douglas to be reversed: in order to understand the recent ethnic violence, it is necessary to instead see the body as 'simultaneously the matrix and the objective of violence' (ibid. 46). That is, according to Appadurai, 'the actual historical bodies fail to observe those same cosmologies that they should represent, and therefore the ethnic body, of victims and assassins, is in and of itself potentially deceptive' (ibid. 74). Violence is then used to 'stabilize' the identity of the ethnic other. I add that violence and torture, which, as Appadurai himself notes, follow fairly identifiable rituals, are used to make the body of the other 'other'.

It is easy to see rituals similar to these being enacted on migrants reaching Italian shores from Africa after perilous journeys on small boats (when they arrive alive, that is). It is first and foremost as bodies that they are dealt with and viewed when filmed for television newscasts. The police, but also medical personnel, whatever their intentions, appear intent on marking them as dangerous bodies, different from 'us', potential bearers of physical, social and cultural 'deviance'. Ethnographies conducted on these shores show the use of immunitarian metaphors, which end up justifying migrants being locked up in temporary detention centres prior to expulsion.

Chapter 3
Prevention and Security

From Criminals to Victims

If preventing is better than curing, it is also better than repressing (and/or punishing). These are two slogans from the 1960s and, in part, the 1970s, that have changed not so much in form, but in substance.

The condition of insecurity, according to Castel (2003), has an existential status that takes on various dimensions depending on the historical period. In the pre-modern age, protection from insecurity was provided by belonging to peasant communities, or, in cities, to corps, guilds, and so on, where the restriction of group norms went hand-in-hand with security. In liberal modernity, insecurity was the condition for the majority of the population, where freedom from ancient constraints produced the dissolution of traditional social ties and had not yet been compensated for by other connections and protections.

The response to the widespread pauperism of the nineteenth century, a generator of insecurity, was the expansion of the state, no longer just a minimal and, simultaneously, police state, but a true and proper risk-reducer, by connecting the status of worker to guarantees and rights. The protective state, the welfare state, was based on the growth of productivity, consumerism, and wages. Its culture was one of progress, of faith in the future. Progress was based precisely on the possibility to plan the future: 'this capacity to master the future seems essential to me from the perspective of a struggle against social insecurity' (Castel 2003: 36).

Furthermore, the social state was based on individuals belonging to protective collectivities: 'the individual is protected thanks to those connections that no longer involve direct participation in "natural communities" (family, neighborhood, etc.) but rather [their participation in] collectivities that are constructed by regulations, and which generally have a legal status' (ibid. 38).

The crisis of the social state, which is simultaneously the crisis of the nation-state, entails deregulation and, along with it, a decline in forms of collective organization. Mass unemployment and the precariousness of labour relations thwart the related employment protections, for which is substituted the promotion of a biographical model: each man and woman must alone assume the risks of their professional journey which has become flexible and disjointed. The future becomes a source of threat and fear, resentment appears as the social response to social malaise, inducing a defensive attitude which rejects, along with innovations, pluralism and differences too, and goes in search of scapegoats.

Therefore, the essence of the slogans from the 1960s and 1970s is very different now than it was then. Preventing is still better than curing, but prevention is no longer above all a social, collective, and institutional duty, but to a great extent, as we have seen, an individual and private one. As regards prevention in the field of deviance and crime, today this is understood above all as a series of policies aimed at making it more difficult to commit crimes, rather than improving the social conditions which, up to very recently, were considered to be the origin of deviance and criminality themselves, and at convincing citizens to take adequate measures to not become victims, or, if they do become them, to reduce the corresponding damage (through the private insurance market).

However, as we will see, while the focus of prevention today has shifted from criminal justice towards other types of public policies, local ones in particular, this does not mean that the criminal policies themselves are relegated to second place. On the contrary, in the last 10 years the prison population of all European countries, Italy included, has grown, not to mention what has happened in the United States where it is calculated that almost four million people, the bulk of whom are African-American and Hispanic, are under the control of the penitentiary authorities (Re 2006).

The question of 'security', in short, is used to justify both policies of prevention, mainly situational, as we will see, and policies of repression, which are in turn justified by an imperative of prevention, which is however different from the classic idea of penalty as mere deterrent. Both are linked by rhetorics which set aside social causes and individual motives that do not have an underlying rational cost–benefit calculation.

In 1985, Cohen (1985) was already talking about the advent of 'administrative' criminal policies and criminological knowledge, thereby intending to indicate the new disinterest in research or intervention on the (supposed) causes of crime. Research and intervention are instead oriented, at least this is the tendency, towards identifying methods to prevent (common) crime, which make extensive use of probabilistic models for determining the salient characteristics of populations 'at-risk' of committing crimes and unlawful acts. These populations will be watched more attentively, and if an individual who possesses some of these characteristics is arrested (typically, it is an African-American or Hispanic young man, unemployed, coming from the inner city, with family problems on his back) he will receive a penalty that is commensurate not with the crime committed, but with the degree of social dangerousness calculated on the basis of these characteristics.

Thus, there is an evident and substantial shift towards a 'criminal law of the author', or even of the 'enemy'; in other words, towards criminal policies and policies of social control that are explicitly geared towards controlling and repressing populations rather than behaviours. The return to centre of the public discourse of the notion of social dangerousness produces policies targeted at defining entire populations, identified on the basis of shared characteristics as bearers of risks and as dangers for 'good citizens'. Thus, it follows that prevention will be connoted as the containment and surveillance of these same populations, rather than as the implementation of policies aimed at decreasing the 'causes' of this alleged dangerousness. A recent example is how the then-French Minister of the Interior Sarkozy labelled the youth of the outskirts of the city as the 'dregs': the problem does not lie in hardship, urban decay, unemployment, and so forth, but instead in 'being' the youth of the outskirts, rabble.

However, the change in relation to traditional positivist criminology, and to the criminal policies it variously inspired, is due to a shift in attention from 'criminal' to 'victim'. The main issue becomes that of diminishing the risk of victimization rather than intervening in the 'causes' of crime. The bulk of current criminological knowledge puts the 'victim' at the centre. Research studies on victimization and on 'fear of crime' are not only the most widespread, but are the studies that are requested or that in any event guide the main trends of criminal policies. The password of national and local governments becomes 'the safety of citizens'; it is a safety that here means being sheltered as much as possible from the risk of being victims of common crimes and incivilities. Today, safety and security in the public discourse mean this, rather than social security, and this is what is provided for through the various preventive measures. In what follows, I will describe this change in more detail along with its consequences, particularly as regards the push towards so-called situational prevention and individual and private prevention.

I won't however dwell here on how crime and deviance, and their perception and social construction have also changed. Certainly, as Marconi notes (2004), the social transformation that goes under the name of post-Fordism, or the end of industrial society, has produced the decline of forms of discipline and social control that were inherent to the Fordist factory and what this implied in terms of the organization of time and space.

Marconi brings to light not only the social control function of the factory as such, but the rigid organization of time and space that its centrality imposed on society as a whole, a rigidity that imposed routine and produced security, not only with respect to the course of life (see, on this, Sennett 1998), but also with respect to the possibility of incurring risks that could make one a victim of crime. The transformation of work, and the fragmentation and precariousness of jobs, in turn, not only implicate the reduction of the social control inherent to the discipline of work itself, but eliminate the separation between different times and spaces of life, increasing, on the one hand, the opportunities for committing illegal acts, and on the other hand, the opportunities for coming into contact with deviant or illegal attitudes (see also Garland 2001).

However, as always, the dynamics of crime and deviance cannot be described without relating them to the change in criminal policies and norms. The most obvious example is the change in norms regarding so-called narcotic substances: an exacerbation of these norms, or simply expanding the definition of illegality to the possession or use of certain substances, very substantially changes the scenario of crime and deviance. Furthermore, the advent of so-called 'zero tolerance' policies for a large number and variety of behaviours that are not illegal, but simply experienced as 'uncivil', expands the field of surveillance, the definition and perception of dangerousness, and therefore also that of deviance, if not of criminality true and proper.

Also, in Europe, and in Italy in particular, anti-immigration policies create an offense out of either clandestine immigration or non-compliance with an order of expulsion from the national territory; this has caused a large number of people who did not commit any type of crime to be imprisoned. In Italy, the prison population is primarily composed of migrants and drug addicts.

From Social Policies to Security Policies

Social control means both the processes that induce conformity and those that repress deviance. These processes are intertwined. As for the former, they include both primary and secondary socialization processes and those processes that in a complex society produce conceptions of what is good and what is bad, of what one can and cannot do. Included among these, as Robert says (2006: 6), is the 'spectacle of control of disorder', which 'constitutes the best pedagogy of an order': the management of disorder serves first and foremost to mark the boundaries of order. The spatial metaphor is not random: the methods of organization and protection of a territory, and first, as the Chicago school has already shown, of the urban territory, must be considered among the processes of social control.

Indeed, as Bauman (2005: 76–77) recently and appropriately notes:

> From the beginning, cities have been places where strangers live together in close proximity to each other while remaining strangers. The company of strangers is always frightening (though not always feared) since it is part of the nature of strangers, as distinct from the nature of both friends and enemies, that their intentions, ways of thinking and responses to shared situations are unknown or not well enough known to calculate the probabilities of their conduct. A

gathering of strangers is a site of endemic and incurable *unpredictability*. You could put it another way: strangers embody *risk*.

Welfare ideology promoted a uniform and morally connoted conception of social life by means of the authority and direction of the (national) state. The main idea was that the social could be governed, reformed, guided by the direct management and intervention of the state in the market, in the economy, through a redistribution of resources intended to diminish the effects of social inequalities.

In terms of social control, understood as a response to deviance, in other words in terms of criminal policies, the prevailing idea in the welfare state was that crime (or more generally, deviance) was the outcome of social or personal shortcomings, at any rate of determinations that at least in part escaped individual responsibility, and which should be remedied by the collectivity through the state and its institutions. At the centre of the punitive ideology of welfare we thus find two interwoven ideas: an improvement of the social conditions that are supposed to lead to deviance (social policies, health and psychiatric policies, understood as either the redistribution of resources in response to social rights or as an investment in the prevention of disorder), and the correction/rehabilitation of the criminal/deviant, through the intervention of expert knowledge (again, social, psychiatric, psychological, criminological), along with the conception of imprisonment as 'good' for the inmate, insofar as it is a place for rehabilitation and correction (Pitch 1995).

In welfare societies, therefore, the dominant paradigms of policies of social control directed at the criminal question were two-fold and intertwined. On the one hand, the idea that deviance and delinquency have social and cultural causes (Merton 1938) legitimized intervention policies that were precisely of the social and cultural type. On the other hand, the idea that deviants and delinquents had inadequately and imperfectly introjected the norms translated to policies of intervention on deviant and delinquent individuals which were aimed at changing their internal motivations (Parsons 1951). What unified the two paradigms was attributing responsibility for deviance and delinquency to the entirety of social relations from which deviants and delinquents drew their motivations to act.

A person who committed a crime, in short, acted 'normally' with respect to the context of opportunities, values, and norms in which that person was inserted, and yet his personal responsibility was in a way limited (Pitch 1995) precisely because his possibilities of choice were limited by this context. The focuses were thus twofold: on the one hand, social and economic intervention, as concerns the context, on the other hand, the intervention of treatment and care of the individual. Penal policies too were reinterpreted according to this rhetoric: the prison must re-educate, rather than punish or neutralize. An entire series of measures accompanied or were substituted for the prison sentence: various forms of probation, early release, and so on.

Nevertheless, prison remained central, not only as the place where failures, e.g., what appeared as irreducible to treatment and care, were unloaded, but also as the more or less recognized driving force of the processes of secondary social control, that which gave them meaning in the last instance.

Indeed, treatment and care agencies worked with a revolving door mentality. Each imposed its own definition of the problem and unloaded elsewhere what did not fall within this definition, producing abundant 'remnants', who for this very reason were reconstructed as untreatable, irreducible, and therefore dangerous.

Starting in the late 1960s in the US, this type of rhetoric began to come under attack from the right and the left. Notwithstanding increasing welfare and the war against poverty of Johnson's presidency, crime rates were rising again (however, see Chambliss 1999, for a contrary reading).

Indeed, as I noted above, the rhetoric of the welfare state found discontents and critics on the left too, who denounced its paternalism, its tendency to pathologize conflicts, and its disregard for the inmates' civil rights.

It is within the welfare crisis and the crises of its cultures that it is necessary to analyse the change in processes of control and the new rhetoric that accompanies them. The crisis of welfare policies brings with it the decline of theories of renewal and reform of the urban and social contexts, as well as of theories of rehabilitation and resocialization. 'Nothing works' becomes the refrain repeated on the left and the right; crime rises, and above all the rate of recidivism, which policies variously inspired by the so-called labelling theories thought they could combat by reducing the effects of the stigma of imprisonment and by keeping the 'deviant' in his social context, when and to the extent this was possible.

First of all, conservative criminologists say, let's leave aside the idea that one commits a crime due to adverse social and environmental conditions. Whoever commits a crime must be considered to be someone who makes a rational choice, weighing the costs and benefits of his action. We should therefore act on the costs, which when increased will make it more difficult to choose to commit a crime. Increasing the costs means relying on criminal repression: increasing the penalties, making them certain (with the introduction, in the US, of mandatory sentencing).

It is the positivist paradigm that is at the basis, in one way or another, of all the theories and analyses of the criminal question since the late nineteenth century, and that is radically put in crisis: the causes of deviance and crime, whether looked for in individual biopsychology and/or in the social context, are put between parentheses. Techniques and strategies of social control begin to be theorized (and practised) independently of enquiries into the presumed causes of the phenomena to be controlled and repressed. The instances of social and moral reform that for better or worse inspired the research into the causes of 'social problems' lose force and meaning in the context of the increasingly larger cuts to social spending, and the complementary emergence of a liberal ideology that thematizes the primacy of private initiative, personal responsibility, individual worthiness and the need for a withdrawal of the state and public intervention that is accused of producing dependency and individual irresponsibility.

The shifting of attention from criminals to victims, the centrality of the notion of risk, the emphasis on the individual and therefore private responsibility (of both the criminal and the victim) are the characteristics of the criminologies that are dominant today, at least in the sense of guiding the rhetoric and, in part, the dynamics of contemporary social control policies. Therefore, theories and policies emerge that change the focus from the individual to populations; from criminals to victims; from a concern about the causes to concern about the consequences: from deviance, control, order to knowledge, risk, security; from concerns that are in some way moral to security concerns; from social prevention to situational prevention (Crawford 1999).

Safety and security, in short, in the sense of being sheltered from the risks of common crime, have become the principal objective and the main subject of criminologies and criminal policies. In this way, problems regarding the quality of life, the crisis of social bonds, the growth in inequalities, the difficulties of relations between people who are bearers of different cultures, are redefined as questions to be faced from the viewpoint of security; we are in the presence, it is said, of a criminalization of poverty (Wacquant 1999).

The question of security, furthermore, is defined as an urban question; that is, it is located in the city. On the one hand, there is nothing new about this, since the big city, as was said above, has been the subject of analyses, concerns, and political experiments as early as the first period of industrialization. Sociologists, politicians, novelists and moralists were all in various ways involved in indicating the dangers (but also the opportunities) of metropolises, dangers that lie in anonymity, in loosening the reins of traditional social ties, in individualism.

Yet, on the other hand, emphases and concerns have changed with the changing of cities. Today, more than half of the world's population lives in an urban or urbanized environment and many cities exceed five million residents. The processes of deindustrialization have hit some cities more than others, producing not only unemployment, but changing the urban physiognomy itself. It is to these processes and to those connected with an increasingly flexible, atypical, and precarious job market that produces segmentation, new inequalities and new poverty, that many attribute the crisis of social bonds, those ties and norms that regulated the daily life of the city and the interaction amongst its residents, and which not least of all were also promoted by major trade unions, mass political parties, and by the associative life produced by these institutions.

The transformations of capitalism moreover implicate a nomadic jumping from job to job and therefore from place to place, making us all internal migrants, barely attached to each place. The rate of trust and solidarity consequently drops, social ties becoming even more precarious.

The relations between city residents are marked by reciprocal disengagement: the *flâneur* of the 1900s has morphed into an indifferent citizen, devoid of curiosity. Impermanence and standardization of consumption produce standardization of the environment and public places without a history or past (major shopping centres, for example, which increasingly become spaces for walking, gathering, spending free time). Public uncertainty pushes withdrawal and investment on family life, which, in turn, leads to civic disengagement (Sennett 2000). But even companies, major multinationals which were at one time active in city life, are today absent from it: they exercise power, but they don't assume civic responsibilities (Sennett 2000).

Furthermore, cities have spatially and functionally extended into the surrounding spaces, the new technologies of communication making it possible to have, on the one hand, further dispersal and suburbanization, and on the other, and complementarily, a revitalization of urban centres either as places for leisure or as sites and shop windows for companies that have in reality spread to more or less everywhere throughout the world. The relationship between centres and outskirts changes and this changes the populations of each of these (Martinotti 1993; Sassen 1994; Amendola 1997). The city is populated not only by those who reside there, but also by whoever goes there to work and returns home elsewhere, and by whoever uses it in their free time, makes use of its resources for pleasure, recreation, and fun, but does not live there. This can cause conflicts between residents and tourists and other 'city users'.

Even so-called multi-ethnicity and multiculturality are more a myth of the cosmopolitan elites than a mass reality. Cultures and ethnic groups live together in metropolises, but rarely mix, producing a public sphere that is based on identity rather than alterity. Reciprocal curiosity gives way to an adaptation through indifference, when not through fear and a defensive attitude: 'In a world of multiplying diasporas, one thing that is not happening is that boundaries are disappearing. Rather they seem to be erected on every new street corner of every declining neighborhood of our world' (Friedman 2000: 141).

Migrants take up residence, according to place of origin, in different areas of the city, usually those where lodging is found at a lesser cost, at cheap boarding houses and motels. This contributes to a further devaluation of that area's real estate and often creates friction and problems with the residents that have been there longer. Similar problems are created in areas that migrants from various cultures choose as privileged gathering places (close to a place of worship, for example, or in the area surrounding a station), occupying spaces that older residents feel are their own.

In relation to these changes, cities and regions today have accumulated new powers and therefore new responsibilities delegated by the national state. The emergence of many major cities as a driving force of economic development and as places where wealth and financial power concentrate further helps to explain why today cities are the focus of policies and concerns, including theoretical ones, about social control, thematized in terms of the citizens' right to security, and how these concerns extend over several fronts, the essential one being that of prevention, the responsibility for which is mainly assigned to the local powers.

Prevention is directed towards potential victims; it puts the victims at the centre of analyses and policies. If the category of oppression was central in welfare, that of victimization is central in post-welfare. The current prevalence of discourses and policies in the name of victimization confuse and retrace the boundaries between what must be considered private and what must be considered public, between public interventions and private interventions. Criminologies on the market today all share the centrality assigned to the notion of risk and the shifting of focus onto victimization.

Victimization revolves around the notion of risk and the problem of how to prevent or reduce it. Most criminologies, to varying extents, focus their analyses on the issue of which measures are more useful for diminishing the risk of becoming victims of crime. Measures of this type are either those geared towards preventing potential criminals from acting (surveillance, zero tolerance, neutralization), or those geared towards making potential victims responsible (don't do this, don't go there, lock up the house well).

The provision that potential victims be attentive is fed into not only by press campaigns, but through booklets and pamphlets published by various urban security offices, which are now widespread more or less everywhere in Italy, and which launch a series of warnings counselling people to: lock the doors and windows of their houses well, install alarm systems, not go to isolated locations, especially at night, not visibly carry cash or wear jewellery, and so on. These precautions make explicit and in some ways imperative what many male, and above all many female citizens already do anyway, *de facto* notably reducing their freedom of movement.

To that end, it is appropriate to analyse a little further the lasting difference between men and women with respect to the ease with which they are allowed to move about urban environments. The research previously mentioned (Pitch and Ventimiglia 2001) brought to light what is after all fairly evident: women are urged to take, and even spontaneously and often routinely and unconsciously do take, an entire series of precautions that men, at least male youths and young adults, don't even dream of adopting. Many locations in the city and many hours of the night are prohibited to women: those who, out of necessity or otherwise, contravene these implicit prohibitions and end up becoming the victims of crimes or incivilities are often 'accused' of guilty imprudence. And indeed, the task of preventing crimes and more common incivilities is still in large part a female task: it is the mothers who try to provide for their sons' and, above all, their daughters' security. More generally, as was said above, it is up to the mothers to educate them in such a way so that the former do not cause trouble and the latter don't get into it.

Many women thus find themselves living in a world that is construed as hostile and threatening; they are urged to avoid not just places, but people too, relationships, to be suspicious and mistrustful of strangers, and in particular of foreigners. In a word, to not take risks, to avoid them. This represents a strong limitation to not only their freedom of movement but also, more generally, their choices with respect to work, free time, travelling and so on compared to the majority of men.

Research has nevertheless shown that it is women who 'take risks' that feel more secure. And women who voluntarily 'take risks' are those that have an adequate store, that is a notable amount, of both economic and social resources and especially cultural resources. The feeling of being in control of one's own situation is crucial here, as Sally Engle Merry (1981) already noted in another study many years ago. And this feeling, in turn, has a lot to do with having those resources that I was talking about (in addition to a familiarity with places and people, which is nevertheless produced through frequentation, not avoidance).

This primarily concerns women, but it also concerns all those people who have insufficient resources to take risks. As it happens, many of them are not even able to put the required precautions into action, since these too cost money (many must be acquired on the market), take time, and require a certain amount of ease. For example, Madriz (1997) shows how it is the poorest women who have to work and travel to places deemed insecure, in some cases even at night, and how, if they are victims of crimes or incivilities, they are blamed rather than helped.

Thus prevention contributes to maintaining and reinforcing inequalities, either because prevention costs, and whoever cannot afford it is implicitly under accusation, or because it is itself a method of discrimination which occurs against weak and vulnerable figures: prostitutes, poor migrants, vagrants, addicts. These people are usually not included among the members of 'society' who are told they are entitled to security, but are instead, as researches indicates, typically cast as figures of 'fear'.

The 'New Prevention': Local Security Policies

> We may say that the sources of danger have moved into the heart of the city. Friends, enemies and above all the elusive and mysterious strangers, veering threateningly between the two extremes, now mix and rub shoulders on the city streets. The war against insecurity, dangers and risks is now waged *inside* the city, and inside the city battlefields are marked out and frontlines are drawn. Heavily armoured trenches and bunkers intended to separate out strangers, keep them away and bar their entry are fast becoming one of the most visible aspects of contemporary cities – though they take many forms and though their designers try hard to blend their creations into the cityscape, thereby 'normalizing' the state of emergency in which the safety-addicted urban residents dwell. (Bauman 2005: 73).

The issue of preventing street crimes and/or victimization from incivility has become a principal issue more or less throughout Europe. There is a European Forum on security that brings together many cities, to which the counterpart organization the Forum Italiano belongs. Security plans have been written and implemented in many Italian cities. We can talk about the security of cities and about security in cities. The former refers to the creation of an environment that is desirable to private investors, attractive to outside capital; the latter refers to the comfort or discomfort of those who live and use the urban space.

I will dedicate a significant space to these policies and the rhetorics that support them, accompany them and justify them, because I think they are essential to understanding how social control is set up today and how 'deviance' is perceived and defined. Furthermore, these policies and the relative rhetorics have effects, often neither foreseen nor desired. On the whole, they go towards legitimizing the current compression of free public spaces in the name of security that is produced by policies implemented to hinder terrorism, and even more so immigration, which, in Italy, is connected more to common crime than to terrorism.

An example that is often evoked of a prevention policy in the name of security is the one Mayor Giuliani implemented in New York. With his 'zero tolerance' catchphrase, Giuliani mobilized the city police on the streets, gave them the task of ridding them of homeless people, beggars, vamps, prostitutes, and street musicians. He intervened by closing the famous red-light locations near Times Square, and gave the police ample power to arrest and lock up anyone suspected of being about to commit a crime or, more simply, an incivility. At the basis of this policy stands the famous 'broken windows theory' (Wilson and Kelling 1982), which says that in a neighbourhood or area where no one is in charge of preventing minor infractions of the law from being committed, or where incivilities are tolerated, such as, the vandalism of abandoned buildings, the activity of graffiti artists and so on, the problems will multiply and gradually become more serious.

> In other words, urban decay would lead to a sense of abandonment in the community, to a lack of attention on the part of the authorities, destined to facilitate deviant behaviors. Decay elevates the threshold of indifference of the urban community towards various forms of deviance, with the dramatic consequence of producing the consolidation of criminal cultures. (De Giorgi 2000: 106)

Actually, this theory does not claim only that there is a need for the 'authorities' to have a visible presence in a given territory: in part contradictorily, it takes up old and known arguments according to which order is based first of all on a community type of control, on forming and maintaining strong and significant social ties. In other words, as Crawford (1999) would later note in regard to British security policies, the 'community' is presented both as the problem and the solution. And in fact, incidentally, these policies are much more successful in places where they are less necessary (well-off neighbourhoods) than in areas where the problems are accumulating and the vandalizing of buildings and urban decay present themselves more as the effects of causes that are complex and originate far away from where they manifested, than as driving forces of deviance and crime in and of themselves.

Using this theory, Giuliani's policy seemed above all to take up the call to bring the police back to its former tasks of controlling and protecting the territory, of ensuring order at any cost whatsoever, thereby displacing the police from its duties of searching for and arresting the perpetrators of serious crimes. New York, rid of its human 'scraps', recorded a spectacular reduction in even violent crimes, drawing new residents, capital and companies, and was proposed as a crime-fighting model, of which the mayor became the symbol.

In fact, as many studies show, a reduction in crime was recorded during the same period, even in cities that did not implement zero tolerance policies, and was probably more connected to the decline in the distribution of crack. The broad powers granted to the police produced very serious abuses, above all, as could be predicted, against members of ethnic minorities.

There is then another, more general consequence that countermarks many urban prevention policies, in Europe as well. As Rose (2000) appropriately notes, the emphasis on incivilities as a sign and symptom of potential deviances and crime shifts the attention of the police and agencies of public order onto these deviances and incivilities rather than onto true and proper illegal acts. Moreover, it is above all the incivilities committed in and by residents of the most degraded areas to be targeted, which leads to these very residents being criminalized, and who by no coincidence usually belong to already discriminated ethnic minorities. Therefore, the association between incivility and deviance leads to the *de facto* intensification of a policy of controlling and repressing people and populations who are identified by a status, belonging to a group, rather than to a policy that represses illegal or uncivil behaviours.

As we will see, this is a fundamental element of how control is set up today in Europe and in Italy in particular, as well as, and indeed especially, through policies against immigration that invent new 'crimes' and illegalities, of which only immigrants themselves can be the perpetrators.

Zero tolerance policies received major publicity and the zero tolerance catchphrase was used in more than one European political campaign, Italy included.

However, the so-called policy of 'new prevention' was not born in the United States, but in France, at least under that name. A history of European local security policies, in addition to the reconstruction by Amendola (2003) is retraced by Robert (2006) (see Amendola 2003) who defines prevention in this way: 'all the non-repressive means for diminishing crime'. From this point of view, social, scholastic and cultural policies can be considered 'preventive' insofar as they pursue this task indirectly, a method, which, as indicated, was preferred during the welfare era.

In Great Britain, in the early 1980s, the current of so-called 'new leftist realists', radical criminologists disillusioned by the results of the previous period, e.g. of policies conducted in the name of the imperatives of decriminalization, deimprisonment and depenalization, and to some extent backed by new movements, like feminism – which brought to light the serious offences and crimes suffered by women – believed that from the viewpoint of a consistently reformist policy it was necessary to take the fear of crime and violence declared by citizens seriously and to make re-establishing legality and security in the poorest areas the centre of this policy (in other words, those areas where street crimes more seriously affected the daily lives of people who were already economically and culturally disadvantaged).

These themes were taken up again by many leftist criminologists in various European countries, Italy included. In other words, the catchphrase of law and order – the weapon of the conservative right – was to be adopted by liberals and used to produce policies that were not merely repressive. Attempts in that direction were made in various cities governed by the Labour Party (even though the central government was solidly conservative).

Robert (2006: 2) nevertheless notes that, in the 1980s, the prevailing model for local security policy in England was one of so-called 'situational prevention'. Robert describes British-style situational prevention as follows: it was based on 'two essential principles: making populations responsible so that they themselves would assume the duties of prevention, and reducing the instances of crime occurring in the environment'. Ultimately, as Robert notes, these policies translated to a strong development of surveillance, first with Neighbourhood Watch programs, and in more recent years with video surveillance. While different from the prevention plans of the new leftist realists, these policies, like those plans, shifted the attention from potential criminals to potential victims.

In France, after the uprisings which broke out in 1981 in a Lyon suburb, a mayors' commission was established, and headed up by Gilbert Bonnemaison. Its plan provided for a so-called 'social' prevention, understood as a policy directed at those areas where there were more social problems, by 'multiplying the interventions there' (Robert 2006: 4) through a complex organization that involved various participants: municipal committees, local state services, associations, and a national committee with representatives from the major administrations. Thus was born the so-called city policy, a set of diverse initiatives directed at intervening in urban decay, scholastic dispersal, juvenile unemployment and so on, through contracts between local powers and prefectures, a policy which somehow moved forward throughout the 1990s, and survived, albeit with significant modifications, changes in the national government.

Before returning to the evolution of the two European models discussed by Robert, it is necessary to further examine the two ways in which prevention is defined.

The first tries to combine some type of social security along with a security that more accurately refers to the risk of crime. The second defines security primarily as prevention of the risk of being victims of crime. In order to describe the latter, I'll rephrase the words of one of its supporters (Felson 2003): situational prevention does not want to change people, nor change the general situation. It is cheap; neither the culture nor the 'general structure' changes. This entails thinking 'practically' rather than 'politically'. It adopts strategies directed at diminishing the benefits of the crime and raising its costs and risks. As is seen, it is a type of prevention that programmatically ignores the past and turns to the future. It does not look at motivations, but at future behaviours. Surveillance and sterilization of the territory are the most commonly adopted strategies. The question, according to Felson (2003), is posed in these terms: it is enough to prevent crimes in certain areas as this does not necessarily cause predatory crime to move elsewhere because it is particular areas that attract crime. Therefore, if crimes are prevented in this zone, is it probable that they will not be committed elsewhere either (for the various definitions of prevention, see Selmini 2004).

Underlying this type of strategy is a criminology that considers the commission of crimes to be a routine and normal event of daily life. This type of criminology states that whether a crime will or will not be committed, whether one will or will not be the victim of some crime, depends on the situation and the opportunities (for a description, see Selmini 2004). It thus concerns arranging things in a way so that we are not victims and/or to make committing crimes in certain areas difficult and not very profitable (Selmini 2000). An integral part of this way of understanding the criminal question involves passing on the bulk of the responsibility of not being victims to the citizens themselves, as I have already noted several times.

Social-communitarian prevention conversely refers to more traditional etiological theories of crime, be they social or individual. It thus adopts measures of intervention in social and cultural situations that are considered to be at greater risk of producing illegal and uncivil phenomena, from attempting to improve urban and residential decay and situations of major social hardship, to providing conflict resolution at the local level, all the way to measures directed towards individual groups such as youths. More precisely 'community prevention' is said to be the kind of prevention that uses primary social control production or reproduction methodologies by mobilizing residents and their associations.

Social-communitarian prevention is distinguished from 'general' social policies in the sense that it is directed at particular populations and/or particular urban areas, or, like the majority of social assistance interventions, is directed at the single individual. Furthermore, it is directed more towards potential victims than potential criminals.

Robert (2006) further states that the two models of prevention – the first traceable to a British practice, the second to a French one – have, over the years, grown closer and closer to one another, ultimately becoming a mix of both 'social' and 'situational' interventions, while the situational aspect is now the prevalent and dominant one.

In Italy, the experiment of Safe Cities, sponsored by the Emilia Romagna region in the early 1990s, was promoted by a group of criminologists, regional officers and the active participation of a member of the state police, and had a perspective close to that of the so-called British leftist realists, and a view towards achieving a reform of the state in the federalist sense and, complementarily, a profound change in the organization of the police. With respect to the British leftist realists, while they shared the concern that the rhetoric weapon of security would be used by the right, they were more wary of attributing fear and insecurity in cities to only, or even primarily, the incidence of common crime and incivilities. In Emilia Romagna the issue instead appeared in those years to consist of producing plans and policies that allowed old and new urban conflicts to be governed without resorting to purely repressive resources. There were however, even within the regionally subsidized scientific committee that was established, significant differences in interpreting what prevention consisted of and how it should be understood, to what insecurity referred, and what the duties were of, on the one hand, researchers, and on the other, administrators (see, too, Selmini 2003).

Yet the fact remains that the catchword of security as a 'new' right of citizens was appropriated by a growing number of municipal and regional administrations, regardless of their political affiliations. It can be supposed that this depended both on the new visibility of mayors I talked about, as they became the recipients of requests that previously had other interlocutors, or rather, together and complementarily, on the propagandist and political force of the demand for security.

Therefore, in those years, in different ways and with different instruments, the security issue (understood as a sheltering from the risks of becoming a victim of crime and incivility) gave birth to *ad hoc* municipal offices, or in any event to projects and actions more or less everywhere throughout Italy.

Rossella Selmini (2000) took a census of and analysed the preventive actions of Italian cities from 1993 until 1999, and found that, as concerns situational prevention, the cities primarily used the municipal police and issued a series of ordinances and warnings: anti-prostitution ordinances, ordinances against illegal trade, ordinances to empty illegally occupied locations or areas, guesthouse controls, and so on. There was, moreover, a large and growing use of surveillance systems with closed-circuit television cameras, above all in public places like parks and squares, but also in schools, historical centres, parking lots. Measures regarding street furniture were also used in order to control people's movements: fencing, blocks of cement, anti-graffiti paint, bench removal. According to this study, situational prevention measures were the most widely used, independently of the city's government coalition.

As for social-communitarian prevention, it is nevertheless different from traditional measures of assistance and social service. First of all, indeed as I was saying, it is directed at particular groups or areas. Second of all, its purpose is directed more to the victims of crimes or potential crimes than the perpetrators. For example, damage reduction measures for drug addicts, accompaniment and assistance services for members of at-risk groups (senior citizens, children, women), psychological assistance measures for those who have suffered a crime, as well as 'self-protection advertising campaigns' form an integral part of this. Many city programs in Selmini's 2000 survey include methods for contributing to commercial practices for the purchase of surveillance systems (called 'means of passive defence').

These campaigns, promoted by local governments, go in the direction of a growing privatization of security. Indeed, the security market we talked about above is growing, and is doing so moreover because the local governments themselves are good clients of this market because they purchase various video surveillance systems. The exponential increase in private security and private police forces is another phenomenon that goes in this same direction.

The schedules of activities of the cities, provinces and regions recorded in the *Forum italiano per la sicurezza urbana* (Italian Forum Association for Urban Safety), published in 2000, indicate a desire to intervene in a complex manner in areas which many of these same schedules regard as not really being at risk of common crimes and incivilities: a distinction is drawn between 'objective' security and the perception of insecurity, but the measures proposed don't seem to take this distinction into account.

In a study on the towns and cities of the Marche region (Giovannetti and Maluccelli 2001), the majority of mayors appeared to be aware of the fact that the insecurity of their own residents had less to do with crime and incivility than with social and cultural changes of a broad scope, in particular the entry of migrants into their areas, and with the mistrust and conflicts that this introduction of new and different people entails. However, the adoption of systems and measures for preventing people from becoming a victim of crime seemed to be their principle response, although not the only one, as if the pressure, and primarily the political-electoral pressure, was too strong to resist. It can also be supposed that it is relatively easier to find resources under the rubric of 'security measures' than for other purposes which are then introduced within these programs. For example, many of the security measures propose interventions of cultural and social mediation with regard to male and female migrants.

Nothing can be said about the results of these measures, neither from the viewpoint of their actual diminishment of street crimes and incivilities nor from that of an increased perception of security on the part of residents, because there is still no research of this kind. What can be said is that in recent years, cities' preventive actions have been multiplying, and everywhere there is a prevalence of situational-type measures, which are precisely those measures that are preponderant and dominant in the political discourse. Even so-called social prevention is being transformed, becoming 'more localized and emergency-oriented'.

In a recent report, Selmini (2006), after a subsequent examination of the new projects underway, confirmed the trend towards situational prevention already noted in the previous analyses, and therefore the definitive defeat of the theories that had brought to life not only Safe Cities, but also many of the local projects of the 1990s. In short, we may note how a security discourse connoted by the surveillance and sterilization of the territory was greatly more effective than the one characterized by social and 'community' intervention.

Yet this shift was already amply inscribed in those experiences (Pitch 2001a; 2001b) as, on the one hand, certain situations of hardship were not able to be confronted and managed locally and, on the other hand, the emphasis on security produced the perverse consequences of multiplying the very demand for security, casting blame onto scapegoats such as immigrants. The political and cultural context of these years – in fact, a context that I already extensively described – and which in Italy has been exasperated by a right-wing government, of which the Lega is a powerful component, was unfavourable to practices of prevention that were, so to speak, solidaristic, non-exclusionary.

More meditated reflections – supported as they are by long-standing experiments – come from Great Britain where Tim Hope (2003) has noted an increase in the emphasis on the roles of individual residents in avoiding the risks of crime. Consequently, he notes a significantly unequal distribution of security, which is only accessible to those who have the means to acquire it, either by purchasing private insurance policies or by choosing to live in 'secure' areas which can be made more secure through private surveillance or by enclosing them (as is the case in gated communities).

Crawford's (2001) detailed analysis of the developments in British security policies in recent years meanwhile notes a continuity between those policies introduced by Conservative governments and those of Labor governments, with the policies of both parties based on delegating tasks that formally fell to the state to partnerships between local governments, citizen organizations and private companies. The enormous increase in the situational-type private security market is one result of this. 'The British Private Security Association is proud that video surveillance has now become acceptable and permanent in society, with a growing market of more than 253 million pounds, and that, on any given day in Great Britain we are being scrutinized by eight different video cameras' (ibid. 437).[1]

Yet Crawford also notes how situational prevention policies, based on individual self-responsibility and supported by criminologies that interpret criminality as a

---

1   The Friday, June 30, 2006 weekly edition of *La Repubblica* has a list of Italian cities with the number of closed-circuit television cameras per number of residents alongside them. Fifty cities were surveyed. The highest number of television cameras, proportionally, is – who knows why – in Reggio Emilia: a good 652 residents per television camera (Rome, to give you an idea, is at the bottom of the list, with 20,498 people per television camera). The newspaper article says: '... television cameras don't only peep at squares, monuments, historical buildings, streets and parks, but gradually expand their scope of action' (Di Bella 2006: 31), being installed at hospitals and even in funeral parlours. '"The new frontier is onboard video surveillance: television camera systems onboard means of transportation, like trains, buses and subways", explains Nicola Girardin, head of Siemens Security' (ibid. 31). In short, the surveillance market 'has become a 1,650 million euro monster'.

normal routine event of daily life, coexist with repressive policies, enacted by the state itself, according to which criminality is conversely an extraordinary event, different from other 'disastrous' phenomena, and must therefore be confronted with rigidity and firmness.

The interpretations of what has happened in French cities also differ. Here too, security policies have undergone changes and oscillations, depending on the government which was first socialist and later conservative. Yet the state, which is much more centralist than in Great Britain, never fully delegated its powers. Social prevention has long been a priority objective that goes against Anglo-American-type situational prevention, concentrating on what has been called city policies; nevertheless, above all in recent years, the shifts in security are evident and strong (Body-Gendrot and Duprez 2001).

Some students maintain that local French security policies have had the effect of improving the residential environment as generally understood in all aspects, from both the social and cultural viewpoints. Others are, however, more perplexed, noting how the problems in poor targeted areas are not local in origin, but national and transnational, and therefore unable to be helped by these policies. Widespread unemployment, the precariousness of the little work there is, and ravaged schools cannot be covered by local policies which by their intervention risk further stigmatizing the urban area, in addition to channelling resources into a single area that is itself thus indicated as 'dangerous'.

As Castel notes (2003: 53): 'staging the situation in the outskirts of cities to be places where there is insecurity is in some way a return to dangerous classes, that is the crystallization in particular marginal groups of everything a society has that is threatening'.

In short, there is a very concrete risk that, rather than dedicating resources to the overall improvement of the social situation and the effective revitalization of the territory, even with residents' contributions, the security rhetoric will become a reality in measures that are exclusively or primarily of the situational prevention type and which end up producing new inequalities and new discriminations in relation to what is actually declared to be a priority today, that is the citizens' right to security.

Following the November 2005 revolts in the outskirts of many major French cities (and not only there), this risk seems to have been proved real. The very issues of inequalities and discrimination, until then put into parentheses, finally appeared in the journalistic debate that followed the revolts.

The coexistence of situational prevention policies and clearly repressive policies is not limited, as noted, to Great Britain, but seems to be typical of a good part of Europe, not to mention the United States. While some (for example, Crawford 2001) see contradictions between these two policies, to me it seems instead that they complement one another in that both put the emphasis on security (as for the duality between managerialism and moralism, see below).

Good practices, although implemented in various European cities, Italy included (see the Prin (Progetti di Interesse Nazionale) 2003 study[2]), seem to have little to do with security, but instead, as noted, using this name in order to ensure financing. Indeed, as noted by Prina (2006), who, while disputing that these experiences have for the most part been ruinous or have produced the perverse effect of multiplying security requirements, acknowledges the fact that in Turin, a city where many good practices have been implemented, it was the 2006 winter Olympic Games that truly transformed the residential climate. This event revitalized the city, took male and female residents out of their houses, put them in contact with others, produced a generalized trust, and effectively put fear and mistrust towards whoever 'is not like us' in check, at least temporarily.

---

2   The 2003 Prin research project consisted of four units, in charge of the universities of Bologna, Padua, Turin and Perugia respectively, which, using different methodologies, analysed various subjects within the common issue of Italian local security policies.

Chapter 4

The Current Dimensions of Social Control

Control and Self-Control

Emphasizing security produces the perverse effect of multiplying the demand for security. The current invasiveness of the ideology or culture of prevention refers back to the idea of a world that is knowable and controllable, and to the utopia of absolute protection and total security. These are very dangerous myths since life is in and of itself risky and taking risks is an indispensable ingredient for producing trust and trust in oneself. Furthermore, the effectiveness of technologies and instruments of prevention is very limited, such that emphasizing it is destined to produce delusions and further insecurity (see Castel 2003).

This emphasis can also be interpreted in another way, i.e. as a method of control that is achieved by generalizing a principle of precaution that must entail the actions of each and every man and woman. It's an internalized method of control, which becomes self-control, and perpetuates the illusion of individual freedom, of having and keeping life in one's own hands. Because, I repeat, if something distinguishes the imperative to prevention today, it is that it is mostly individualized and privatized, and concerns individual bodies and individual situations rather than the social causes of ills and hardships. It requires actions and choices that are themselves also individualized and privatized.

The protagonism assigned to 'victims' and the current centrality of the thematic of victimization signify and reinforce it. First of all, focusing on victims or potential victims tends to shift the attention from past to future, from intervening in the (supposed) social causes of hardships and street crime to preventing the risk of being victims of these things. It then bases agency and protagonism on the status of being a victim or potential victim. This is a method of empowerment that appeals to vulnerability, fragility, fear. Lastly, it combines widespread and impersonal methods of control with the call to individual prevention. Everyone must act so as not to become victims, or take precautions to minimize the damage if they do become victims. A city under surveillance (which I will discuss later) appears to be populated by individuals who in turn self-supervise, forming a spiral of reciprocal mistrust that produces further privatization or closure in 'complicit communities'.

Self-responsibilization as a method of control seems to be nothing new, since self-control has been viewed as the other side of control as early as Mead (1967), as well as, naturally, by Freud and then Foucault (1975). But in the context of a cultural domination of the imperative of prevention, and of a privatized and individualized prevention, self-responsibilization assumes the connotation of discriminating between the good citizens, who can take care of themselves by themselves, and the others, the marginalized, the excluded.

There are other consequences for the centrality of victim status and victimization processes in security policies. In addition to clearly simplifying the criminological discourse – I would say, from this viewpoint, even returning to the most reductive positivism (because the production of criminality and deviance can and must also be viewed from the standpoint of the social construction of problems, while the attribution and assumption of victim status is not queried in this way, seeming to be merely the result of having suffered some crime or damage) – they lead to concentrating one's attention on so-called petty crime. Petty crime is an illegality that victimizes not just individuals, but specific ones to the detriment of that illegality, which conversely strikes in a widespread and not directly visible way, for example economic or organized crime (in Italy, as everybody knows, organized crime is very strong and diffuse). This is usually the case with major crimes, whether they are crimes of 'the powerful' or organized crimes, both of which are now more than ever thriving in the deregulated transnational space and are outside the scope of the national government's control. This is one of the more critical points of the rhetoric of security, to the extent that it contributes to shifting the attention towards containing and controlling groups and individuals that belong to particular populations already at the margins of social life, and construed as true and proper scapegoats for the diffuse experience of insecurity (Ruggiero 2004).

In turn, the nearly exclusive attention to petty crime and incivility leads to widespread surveillance policies and territorial sterilization, which are not only in and of themselves discriminatory, but dangerous for the freedom and civil rights of all.

A result of the emphasis on victimization is also the dissemination of rhetorics and practices of mediation in which victims are supposed to play the roles of protagonists. As for criminal mediation, which was experimented with in the Italian youth justice system, in addition to privatizing criminal justice, it risks moralizing justice itself since mediation must induce if not repentance (although there is this too), at least a conscious assumption of responsibility by the offender for the damage caused. I will return to this issue later.

The social mediation of conflicts is explicitly indicated as an important, if not fundamental, component of local security policies. To that end, professional training courses for mediators are multiplying, thereby representing the progressive institutionalization, with its normative correlations, of a practice that wants to be fluid, geared towards simply inducing self-responsibility and protagonism in people who are directly involved in conflicts. On the one hand, beyond its effectiveness, the spread of mediation signals the loss of social and personal instruments for facing conflicts. On the other hand, it signals the increasingly accentuated trend towards problematizing daily life. In this sense, and insofar as experts in mediation are proliferating, self-responsibility and conflict management risk turning into a renewed dependency on the knowledge and actions of someone else. Perhaps social mediation is today one of the few available strategies for attempting to reconstruct social ties in a certain zone or situation; however, it is a strategy that risks excluding the social and economic causes of conflicts, concentrating on cultural and normative differences rather than on inequalities.

Surveillance

Security policies, as I have said, make extensive use of surveillance and territorial sterilization systems. Yet these practices are in turn only one part of the measures made possible by new technologies.

In a recent book, Lyon (2001) delineates the various methods and analyses the consequences of a society of information being at once, and complementarily, a society of surveillance. For Lyon, the principal issue is that the disappearance of bodies and their increasing nomadism combine to prevent the trust and control that was inherent in their visibility and presence. Trust then is delegated to the possession of a range of instruments of identification, from credit cards to genetic testing, which simultaneously are, or function as, impersonal instruments of control. Rather than being managed by a single agency, they are scattered between both public and private agencies, whose data collection is nevertheless always subject to being centralized, and in any event circulates from one agency to the next: 'In our nomadic world, the society of strangers seeks privacy that actually gives rise to surveillance. Tokens of trust, such as personal identification numbers and bar-coded cards, are demanded to demonstrate eligibility or reputation' (Lyon 2001: 27). Therefore, as Rodotà notes (2001), there is a trend towards obtaining absolute transparency, an old dream of all totalitarianisms.

Behind these measures is the need for governing risk, the desire to reduce uncertainty and to control unforeseen events, not only as concerns all of the issues we might summarize under the rubric of 'law and order', but also, and perhaps above all, in sectors of the market economy. 'Rather than producing for an uncertain market, companies now attempt to customize, to cater for discrete markets to create the consumers they need' (Lyon 2001: 48). The new individualized production needs to control, and in some way even construct, the consumer.

Yet in regard to credit risk, there is also a need to establish who is a reliable individual. A very important role is performed by insurance companies, whose *modus operandi* has an influence not only on the economic sector, but also on the social sector since their decisions have a strong impact on people's life opportunities. Increasingly often, insurance companies make decisions based on information that is used to establish the degree of risk represented by individuals. On the one hand, this is information that may come from data collected by other agencies such as the police; on the other, it in turn circulates in the most diverse of databases.

It is precisely the formation of synergies between different public and private agencies, through the effusion and communication of people's data from one database to another, that creates a network of widespread and penetrating surveillance that is geared towards governing and preventing all kinds of risks. It is an activity that is programmatically turned towards the future, and which complementarily ignores the past. What counts, for the purposes of preventing future risks, are the signs, the 'traces of bodies' that we leave in the present.

A privileged place for performing this surveillance is the city. The city is continuously monitored by computer systems that are not limited to closed-circuit television cameras. Informational cities, for which the video game SimCity is a metaphor, regulate daily life, making it so that each person is at the right place at the right time, 'traveling at the right speed or carrying the correct items' (Lyon 2001: 51). The purpose, Lyon states, is not so much to seize the current event, but to anticipate actions, to plan for every eventuality. Electronic simulation allows for the preventive determination of behaviours and the related precautionary actions. What is interesting is not what we do, but what we will do or say.

It is a surveillance that confirms age-old social discriminations and inequalities and creates new ones. To be or not to be in possession of instruments that prove we are reliable, to be or to not be able to be insured against certain risks, and to be or to not be hired for a certain job are increasingly questions that depend on the collection and interpretation of data obtained by computer or, worse, from genetics and biometrics which are used to construct the risk 'profiles' represented by each person.

Prevention operates in various fields and explicitly shows its controlling side. For example, at work: 'Would-be workers are checked for propensities and inclinations, for early warning signs, rather than for what they have actually achieved ... Thus workers who may become pregnant or those susceptible to certain diseases may be disqualified for employment' (Lyon 2001: 41). Added to anti-drug and AIDS testing is genetic testing, which is used to try to predict the emergence of illnesses that could render workers unusable in the future.

In the city, new 'global elites' can create their own separate world thanks to the wealth of information they possess, and thus isolate themselves by excluding everyone else: 'Fear generated divisive architectural policies that turned inward and backward rather than facing the actual social challenges of urban life. Fear may be met with turns to an idealized past, to a fantasy world' (Lyon 2001: 58), sometimes artificially recreated in thematic malls, in separate and supervised neighbourhoods and gated communities.

In the city, therefore, inequality is strongly affirmed and reinforced by preventive surveillance measures, which include electronic barriers and ensure the concurrence of official police activities and those of an increasingly growing private police force:

> The architecture of fear and intimidation spills over urban public spaces, transforming them tirelessly though surreptitiously into closely guarded areas controlled round the clock ... Nan Ellin names a few devices, mostly American in origin, but widely emulated – like 'bum-proof', barrel-shaped benches combined with sprinkler systems in Los Angeles city parks ... or sprinkler systems combined with an ear-splitting racket of mechanical music to chase loafers and loiterers away from the surroundings of convenience stores. (Bauman 2005: 74).

Indeed, even the *modus operandi* of the police has changed significantly with the adoption of new technologies. The tendency to construct risk profiles for individuals and populations that are to be kept under control before they commit crimes is reinforced by these very technologies.

By profiling I mean 'the recording and classification of personal behaviors' (Bonacchi 2003). This is not, in and of itself, a new technique: one of the first profiles was the one delineated by the autopsy report done on the last victim of Jack the Ripper. And profiles were constructed of Hitler in order to try to predict his moves, and more generally, in the US, of other 'enemies' of subsequent wars, naturally including those contemporary ones. One characteristic of profiling for criminological use is the construction of models of behavioural prediction for individuals based on signs, traces left on bodies from crimes or surrounding them, through which the personality of whoever committed those crimes is reconstructed in a laboratory. It is clear that profilers are not interested in social causes, or in the deep motivations for the crime itself. What they are interested in is, precisely, constructing a model of prediction of future behaviour in such a way so as to predict and prevent it. The individual thus reconstructed does not have depth, as he has neither a past nor significant social relations.

Today, laboratory techniques make use of discoveries in the fields of genetics and information technology. Biometrics and genetics imply a method of surveillance through traces left by bodies, but in which concrete people disappear. The body is used as a source of data, chopped up, fragmented, deprived of consciousness and sociality. It is not the body in its entirety and concreteness that is of interest, but parts of the body itself which are interpreted as data: hair, blood, skin, urine, are offered up for analysis in order to organize and classify, to predict and prevent, to construct risk profiles. Bodies become identification documents: eyes, hands, voices become instruments through which access to certain areas or to certain services is granted or denied. In the final analysis, 'body surveillance is consistent with the emergence of a behavioural approach that cares more about the prevention of certain behaviours than their causes, or the social conditions that gave rise to them' (Lyon 2001: 75). Biological reductionism and genetic determinism compete to thwart the importance of both individual biography and the networks of sociality through which personal identities are constructed.

The success of certain contemporary films and fiction brings to light this tendency. *Minority Report*, *CSI*, *Gattaca* and *The Silence of the Lambs* are all based on the protagonists' construction of risk profiles or techniques for predicting behaviours based on traces, signs, tracks left by bodies, where deeper motivations or social causes are not important, and where, on the contrary, there is an insistence on a sort of behavioural determinism that can be interpreted through these signs and tracks.

'Minority Report Syndrome' is the title of an article by Giuseppe D'Avanzo in *Repubblica* (April 3, 2004: 32) commenting on a rash of preventive arrests of 161 Muslims residing in Italy. The question of terrorism will be examined later, along with that of war, but it is evident that in a context like the current one, preventive measures are destined to become more and more frequent and expansive. In regard to people who are suspected of possibly having some kind of contact with terrorism that is Islamic fundamentalist in origin, civil rights and the very guarantees of the rule of law are suspended, and rather than proceeding judicially, steps are taken administratively. D'Avanzo says 'If it is hypothesized that, by removing the suspects, the danger will be cancelled out, the limit of this same conception of legitimate defense before a specific, current, unavoidable danger is pushed back from a judicial dimension to a pre-judicial territory' (2004: 15). And the head of police, De Gennaro, was quoted as saying: 'Our action is geared towards thwarting those who are suspected of gravitating to the area that is closest to fundamentalism. It's a preventive action for which there is no certainty as concerns everything that may have been averted' (2004: 15).

The growing availability of technologies of control, Rodotà says (2006), pushes towards the direction of a 'definitive expropriation of life'.

> Even if comprehensive and global surveillance plans are still not a reality, the critical point consists of going from one representation of reality to another, from ascertaining that yesterday's exceptionality has become today's 'normality'. The crowd is no longer 'solitary', and therefore immune from ongoing social

scrutiny. It is now 'naked', defenseless before the public or private presumption of an ongoing generalized control. This nudity finds growing support in digital technology which, in the stream of images recorded by the most diverse systems of video surveillance, allows a face to be identified without difficulty, and therefore moments and places of public presence for each person to be rediscovered. The freedom of circulation, still proclaimed by constitutions, is vanishing. (Rodotà 2006: 105)

The research on these trends has led many, including some criminologists, to conclude that today the moral discourse on deviance has been entirely translated into a 'utilitarian morality of probability calculus … gutted of moral wrongdoing, deviance is treated as a normal occurrence … a contingency for which there are risk technologies to spread loss and to prevent recurrence' (Lyon 2001: 83; see, too, Lianos and Douglas 2000). That's why many criminologists talk about actuarial criminal policies, tinged by criminological theories which, as has already been noted, abandon the positivist paradigm of researching the causes, be they individual or social, of illegal or deviant acts, in order to concentrate on methods to prevent the risk of becoming victims of them.

These trends in the field of crime are nevertheless, as has been seen up to now, much more general and generalized, extending to the surveillance of every man and woman, as, first of all, consumers and workers, and of the entire city. The emergence of terrorism strengthens this trend, as is obvious, which is very dangerous for maintaining civil rights and freedoms.

And yet we have already seen how one cannot talk about a complete demoralization of contemporary social control: prevention itself functions through measures that pass through individual motivations, moulding and influencing them with the call to or the imposition of norms and values that have a moral implication. Self-control and independence are exalted as civic virtues, and if the 'good life', the 'just life may not be inspired by so-called traditional values they are nevertheless proposed as the result of attitudes and behaviours that depend strictly on how much we are able to prevent and control events, that is to individually face adversities. This way of defining individualism, while not new, puts it at the centre of the search for the good life, and therefore makes it a moral imperative.

The rhetorics that legitimize the practices and techniques of mediation, now extended to a broad range of 'social problems' (from criminal issues, to conflicts at school, in the family, or the neighbourhood), claim the virtue of individual responsibility, by activating the capacity for protagonism in resolving conflicts and problems. As far as criminal mediation is concerned, this is not only invoked as a way of facing the psychological and material problems of victims of crimes, but also as a measure that impedes recidivism, that is, prevents the same individual from committing new crimes. By criminal mediation I mean the confrontation between the perpetrator of the crime (the alleged crime, when the mediation, as usually occurs, is prior to the proceeding) and the victim, a confrontation in which a third party – the mediator – who should be neutral and impartial, should act in such a way that a dialogue develops between the two other parties that induces acknowledgment of the damage caused by the perpetrators and their assumption of responsibility for the consequences of their action, along with the complementary reassurance of the victim. The victim comes to be recognized as a concrete person, and, in regard to whoever caused her damage, should or could 'pardon' perpetrators following their 'repentance' and/or their willingness to in some way remedy the damage caused.

There are in reality many different types of criminal mediation, some of which do not necessarily contemplate a direct confrontation between perpetrator and victim, others that have become an integral part of the functioning of the criminal justice system, while still others operate outside of this system. Even the rhetorics that justify them are multiple and diverse. All of them, however, claim the need to make the victim into a protagonist who manages whatever happened to her, and, more generally, to 'return the conflict to its protagonists'. I shall not comment on the definition 'conflict' as that which is legally defined a crime. Rather, I want to highlight the tendency towards making both protagonists – victim and perpetrator – responsible, as well as the frequent claim of the preventive function of mediation with respect to the risk of recidivism. This preventive function relies not only on the formal recognition by the perpetrator with respect to the consequences of his actions, but also, complementarily, on his 'repentance' and assumption of moral values and norms in effect in the 'community' to which he belongs, to which he may therefore return, well accepted and without risking stigmatization.

It seems clear to me that this is a version of control that is hardly 'demoralized'.[1] Indeed, the dissemination of mediation practices and the rhetorics that justify them form part of those techniques of self-government (Rose 2000) that are defined according to the values of independence and autonomy that were discussed previously. The same zero-tolerance policies, indeed, appeal to the so-called 'broken windows' theory which imputes social disorder to a break in the moral capacity of the 'community' to control itself.

Therefore, here too, a re-moralization of social control is underway, through decentralized methods of intervention which seek to appeal to and stir up the

---

1   Extolled and proposed as a measure of reparative justice, mediation seems to me another instance of the privatization of criminal justice, via the protagonism of victims. The liberal justification of penal law attributes to it the task of discouraging the majority of citizens from committing crimes, and the complementary one of preventing individual and private vengeance (Ferrajoli 1989). Neither repentance of the perpetrator, nor satisfaction of the individual victim have anything to do with the liberal paradigm of penal law.

moral feelings of families, neighbourhood groups and schools within a single 'community' (for an interpretation of the ambiguity of this term within British security policies, see Crawford 1999).

Crawford (2001), in assessing the rhetoric and actual impact of British security policies inspired by Blair's (and Gidden's) Third Way, sees a contrast between managerial influences, tinged with an instrumental logic (efficacy), and the emphasis on the community as a place of values and morality. Garland (1996), in turn, distinguishes between a criminology of me and a criminology of the other, both present today, wherein the former sees criminality as an ordinary, routine question and tends to dedramatize it by preaching strategies of avoidance in daily life, while the latter demonizes the criminal, arouses popular hostilities and concerns and seeks to reach a consensus in favour of draconian measures of control. However, as I will argue below, this is a dualism, not a contradiction. Moralization (and dramatization) and managerialism (and dedramatization) coexist, not only in regard to crime, but as more general methods of control of every man and woman.

We all collaborate, both with impersonal and generalized surveillance, by using credit cards, passwords, bar codes and so on, and, obviously, to self-surveillance. This spontaneous collaboration goes under the name of individual freedom; it is the form of this freedom. Being responsible for the choices we must continuously make in daily life and conforming to the imperative of 'doing it yourself' – and preventive practices are an integral and in fact fundamental part of this – are what in our own eyes appears to be freedom.

In the West, we live in the context of a deformalization and a destructuralization of those institutions which until recently had been committed to the normalization and control of the fundamental areas of daily life, legitimized in this task by their simultaneously being distributors of resources and services – of a form of prevention of the collective, social type. Such deformalization is pursued by the cultural domination of neoliberalism in the name of reconquering the good of individual freedom. But a society deprived of *institutional* mediations is a society 'with exposed nerves' (De Leonardis 2001), a society that favours the perception (that can also be emotional) of problems in individual and private terms.

The critique of the social state has not only been done by neoliberal 'right'. The effects of paternalism, depoliticization and pathologization of social problems, of authoritative invasion of 'vital worlds', have also, indeed in particular, been brought to light by the 'left'. This may help explain why certain measures and practices which we talked about here have a 'progressive' connotation. This is the case with mediation, which is often proposed not only as a method of self-responsibilization, but as a way to reconstruct solidary social ties – in families, school, in the neighbourhood. The idea is to build up and make protagonists in the management of conflicts those 'intermediate bodies', lying between the state and the individual, which have been cast aside, impoverished and deprived of power by the intrusiveness of the social state. The 'progressive' prescription for reform of the social state provides for the protagonism of citizens, the collaboration between non-state organizations and state institutions, and ways of finding and distributing resources that appeal to and stimulate individual and collective capacities. However, at least to date, the result of this attempt appears to be the relegation of tasks and duties that were the state's to a private–social sector that not only cannot take them on, but often tries to fulfil them by violating important rights – for example, the right of equal pay for its workers – which are postponed via the justification of operating for the good of those assisted.[2] Complementarily, social rights tend to be transformed into benefits and provisions entrusted to voluntary solidarity or even to the private market and are therefore perishing.

Welfare reform, according to, for example, Sennett (2003), is for the most part defined by the forms and ways in which companies have been reorganized, that is, it is inspired by the criteria of efficiency, cost reduction, the simplification of bureaucracy. Like companies, welfare must thus become 'flat and short'. Yet, 'short welfare which diminishes government responsibility shifts the management of fate back onto the individual. As in flat, short corporations, the result is to create inequalities' (ibid. 187), in particular among users who are more or less dependent on the help they receive. It is those who are the most dependent who receive services of inferior quality. Jessop (1988) remarked that reform, in Great Britain for example, has meant the crisis of the universalistic welfare model, according to which certain benefits are conceived of as rights of all, and which has been ousted by a two-fold policy that grants self-financed bonuses to the privileged and stigmatizing and punitive charity for the less privileged.

Crawford, in regard to the security policies wanted by the British Labor Party, further notes how the insistent call to citizens' duties and responsibilities intentionally silences rights, while partnerships between various agencies of the public, market and third sectors do not distinguish between them (the agencies), generating, at best, confusion, competition, and a multiplication of ultra-professionalized services. Furthermore, 'the question of security and the very essence of interorganizational partnerships confuses the boundaries of the traditional distinctions between what belongs to the criminal justice system and what should be the task of other public administrations' (Crawford 2001: 452). A potential consequence of this is granting crime a central position in the construction of the social order and therefore marginalizing social problems, and considering them

---

2   Robert (2006) talks, in regard to trends in the field of security policies, of the growing production of a new proletariat of unspecialized and badly paid people without recognized social rights, who are assigned to various tasks in the context of these policies by agencies and private organizations that work through partnerships with public institutions.

only and primarily for their crime-favouring qualities: 'The risk is that residential decay, unemployment, low-quality education, etc. be viewed not as problems that are important in and of themselves, but as producers of delinquency and disorder' (ibid. 452), which is equivalent to a 'criminalization of social policies'.

The insecurity this produces is then displaced elsewhere: to common crime, to migrants, but also, and at the same time, to the care of oneself, what is closest to oneself and considered to be one's own. This does not necessarily create order: things can also be governed with disorder, through the imperative of each person taking charge of only that portion of the situation that concerns them directly. Or to put it better, returning once again to the research of Mary Douglas (1992), the imperative to prevention tends to impose a system on an experience that is otherwise entirely disordered. Disorder here means the crisis and potentially the disappearance of that sociality produced through the interaction of the welfare state with collective organizations – parties, trade unions – which were at the same time creators and supporters of the welfare state.

The Security Market Once Again

The private security market, which we have already talked about a little, has to do with the control of disorder, rather than the production of order.

Private security has always existed; and not just prior to the national state's monopolization of legitimate violence. The notion of legitimate defence – the power to defend one's own home, either with alarm systems or by keeping an arm in the house, and, up to very recent times, delegating to the father of the family the responsibility of controlling his wife and children – shows how the production of security by the state has always coexisted with the private production of security. What has today changed is the extension of this market and the synergies that are created between it and the security produced by public institutions. The social demand for security has multiplied hand in hand with the growing privatization of social relations, delineating a significant shift from the state to the market of the relevant shares of security. It is a market that not only includes security, surveillance, production, dissemination of technological instruments of prevention, but also, as already indicated, new professions and resources, such as those relating to conflict mediation.

> The private security market is asked to offer competencies and technologies for the dissemination of a social *panopticon*, a 'free' network of eyes watching over reality, like the Internet. It is not asked to produce order, but the possibility of knowing in advance that disorder will occur. (Pavarini 2001: 14)

American private prisons are part of this market, but Italian therapeutic communities for drug addicts are too, not only because many people have been sent there by judicial order, but also because they perform a *de facto* function of control and 'damage reduction' for those who are considered as dangerous to others as well as to themselves.

Temporary residence centres for migrants are also part of this, because they are assigned to non-governmental organizations or third-sector associations. Bertaccini (2001: 53) refers to these places and measures as 'privatization of elements of the punitive system', reserving for all the others the name of 'marketing of social control' (local security, television surveillance, emergency intervention, transportation of valuables, anti-theft devices, etc.).

Today in Italy alone there are more than 1,100 private security institutions, which employ more than 43,000 guards, and the sector is constantly expanding.

> In order to protect their sites, local governments seek out the joys of the market, either because subcontracting is preferable to increasing a staff that is too costly and too unmanageable for the tasks of surveillance, or because local governments, already linked to the powerful groups they have delegated with the provision of water or waste removal, are bad at resisting the tempting offers of these same groups when they come to sell them security. (Robert 2006: 10)

The private security market contributes to shifting the emphasis from repression onto prevention and it is prevention of a situational type, free of moral or social concerns. Furthermore, it shifts the attention onto the phenomena of petty crime and incivility. Functional as this is for private interests, and managed by them, it accentuates the inequalities of citizens, and not only in regard to the resource of security. Robert (2006: 10) said: 'A gap has emerged between those that can buy the means to protect themselves on the market and the others; between those that can live in protected areas and the others.'

Control and Exclusion

All, as citizens and city users, are at least somewhat involved with impersonal surveillance. Yet self-surveillance, responsibility, the imperative to be independent and the personal assumption of preventive practices seem to above all concern those who are able to do all of these things.

Cohen (1985) has already pointed out how control assumes different forms for the marginal and the middle classes: for the latter, this still occurs through individual motivations and a call to moral values. However, for the poorer and disadvantaged classes, control is carried out through impersonal devices, which are informed by an administrative and actuarial type of rhetoric and are supported by the notion of social dangerousness. The dangerousness of entire populations, he declared, was identified through certain recurring variables.

Today, the dissemination of generalized surveillance techniques treats all men and women as potentially dangerous, but in reality these techniques are performed in a way that precisely identifies and selects particular populations, based not only on their danger, but on their unreliability as concerns the possession of the requirements deemed necessary to have access to private and privatized goods and resources.

It is for this purpose that the by now abused metaphor of exclusion seems useful: these populations literally find themselves barred from accessing the areas, places, times and resources available to others. However, this metaphor loses its explanatory potential when one reflects on the fact that they are not always marginal, and much less so excluded, from the areas of production that are today central, and which are conversely increasingly based on the precarious, flexible, insecure and badly paid work of these very populations. Exclusion, then, is not so much a condition as a strategy or, more accurately, a form of current social control. It governs through, on the one hand, devices that push towards self-surveillance and drip with moral imperatives and, on the other hand, through impersonal dynamics that push towards the exclusion from places, goods and services, but not from the current central areas of production. Exclusion can thus be viewed as a method of governing this new and necessary workforce: prison itself, to reiterate a hypothesis of Melossi (2002), could be interpreted as an 'entryway to citizenship', if we adopt an optimistic viewpoint. In fact, according to Melossi, the current high rate of imprisonment could be analogous to imprisonment during other periods of great change in labour organization, in which the infusion of new workers was viewed with concern by the pre-existing working class which experienced the new workers as 'rogue', 'scum', etc. In time, imprisonment was attenuated insofar as the new working class was stably inserted into the system.

I don't share this 'optimistic' hypothesis (see, too, De Giorgi 2002) because I believe that the transformations underway are qualitatively different from the preceding ones and therefore do not permit, if they are not guided by a policy at the global level that is capable and intentioned, toning down the structurally precarious and temporary nature of the new workforce. And furthermore, as we have seen, it's not just a matter of imprisonment: a growing number of the population (migrants, for example) is subject to measures that lie 'outside of the law' – in which prison, however, still plays a part.

Anyway, exclusion used as a method of social control for these 'new' populations, who are necessary for contemporary production, whether provisional or not, seems to be the current form of governing them. It is a type of governance that affirms itself through an exclusion produced by surveillance technologies along with, nay complementarily with, the trimming down of the social state and the loss of force of its institutions, by isolating these very populations, keeping them weak, ghettoizing them, imprisoning them, in a word keeping them outside the door of full social citizenship. Not to mention the concealment of what ties the 'included' to the 'excluded' (for which the metaphor of exclusion is itself a method): inequalities, power, hierarchies. It is thus not always a matter of 'excess population' in the sense of the unemployed and the unemployable. On the contrary, this often concerns the employed workforce, particularly those employed in the central sectors of contemporary production of the globalized world, if only in the atypical ways that are now prevalent.

Self-surveillance and exclusion are then two complementary methods of control, as are impersonal surveillance and intervention through individual motivations and moral imperatives, not to mention the 'new prevention' policies on territory and prison.

The decline of social prevention and the emphasis on individual and private prevention contribute in a way that is of capital importance to these outcomes, which converge in social fragmentation and dispersal. In short, this leads to an individualization that not only tends to isolate everybody in their own selves, but tends to construct non-individuated individuals, if we can put it like that: that is, 'individuals' that are not only abstract, but fragmented, without roots, without a body, empty inside. The equivalent of this form of individuality is what I was talking about before, a freedom without content, nomadic in the sense of being able to or having to wander incessantly between places and thus ephemeral choices, connoted by insecurity and lacking true autonomy.[3]

---

3 Benasayag and Schmit (2004: 101), who have already been cited often in these pages, recall how Aristotle 'contradicting common sense, explains that the slave is he who has no ties, who does not have his own place, who can be used everywhere and in various ways. The free man is instead he who has many ties and many obligations towards others, towards the city and towards the place in which he lives.'

Chapter 5
Prevention, Politics, Law

Preventive War

The justification of preventive war is no different from that of the war against crime. In both cases, security is at the centre. Furthermore, such justification makes use of the current blurring of the distinction between the internal enemy – the criminal – and the external enemy – the foreigner. Dangerous 'die-hard' criminals are identified based on certain characteristics that thus enable entire populations that are 'at risk of committing crimes' to be identified. It is no different for enemies: they, in reality, are criminals or potential criminals, and are identified based on characteristics that select states and even peoples (e.g. 'Islamic integralists', a metonym for Arabs) as being at 'risk of committing hostile acts against us'.

Clearly what interests me here is the rhetoric that justifies preventive war, not its 'real' reasons. The rhetoric is interesting because it is used to seek a consensus, an important and even decisive issue for unleashing a war, especially in a democracy.

This particular justification, used in the war against Iraq, makes use of stylistic features that have by now become common sense and which were reinforced by the shock of September 11th, a shock that highlighted the 'reasonableness' of fear and insecurity, and the fact that they are related to threats that come from both inside and outside. September 11th was used to show that it is impossible to distinguish inside from outside, as boundaries are permeable and the 'enemies' become confused with us. War, paradoxically, lists among its tasks that of restabilizing boundaries, drawing a separation between us and them, between inside and outside.

The construction of criminals as enemies possessing certain particular characteristics serves the same function: they are 'different', and therefore threatening. The question of security is thus played out in an attempt to move the danger outside, to identify it, to make it visible. War, in this context, and in particular preventive war, yields to the function of attenuating the sense of insecurity that derives from the perception of being the enemy among us, of being 'us', through the invention of an easily identifiable scapegoat. And, if such a scapegoat is not identifiable, then the war itself makes it so, inscribing its diversity from 'us' onto its own body: bombarding it, killing it, torturing it. The rituals of degradation of Abu Ghraib have this sense.

There are at least two types of 'new' wars. The first is the one analysed by Mary Kaldor (2006), and she contends that it has the following characteristics: they are not fought between states; their purposes have to do with the politics of identities, rather than with the ideological counterpositions of the past; they are primarily fought using guerrilla methods, but, unlike in the past, these methods are used against the local populations for the purpose of 'ethnic cleansing'. The troops in the field are a mixture of paramilitary units, war lords, criminal gangs, mercenaries, organizationally decentralized and often in contrast with one another. These are the wars to which I referred, which are tinged by a defensive invention of the past, where ethnic cleansing must produce, through the destruction of bodies or their 'use' (the practice of so-called 'ethnic rape'), a 'pure' identity that is consistent with the 'original' one yearned for.

Then there are the so-called asymmetrical wars, fought by powerful and well-armed states against much weaker ones, a relevant characteristic of which is the use of arms that avoid direct contact between the former and the latter's soldiers whenever possible. This, Rodotà notes, entails concealing another disturbing body (in addition to those of women), by virtue of the use of advanced technologies:

> The enemy's body is increasingly hidden from the eyes of the combatant. Intelligent arms identify the target from a distance, see in the dark, guide bombs and projectiles. The body to be struck becomes not only invisible, but even unrecognizable: and electronic war thus assumes the abstract characteristics of a video game. The exclusion of the body contributes to excluding movements of consciousness, knowledge of the action. Will the torments that accompanied the life of the pilot of the *Enola Gay*, the airplane from which the atomic bomb was dropped on Hiroshima, still be possible? (Rodotà 2006: 97)

More generally, Bauman (2004: 75) says:

> One of the most sinister effects of globalization is the deregulation of wars. Most present-day warlike actions, and the most cruel and gory among them, are conducted by non-state entities, subject to no state laws and no international conventions. They are simultaneously outcomes and auxiliary but powerful causes of the continuous erosion of state sovereignty and the continuing frontier-land conditions in the 'inter-state' global space. Intertribal antagonisms break into the open thanks to the weakening hands of the state, or in the case of the 'new states', of hands never given time to grow strong.

Naturally, there is also transnational terrorism, the definition of which is the subject of conflicts, since it is confused with guerrilla warfare and often uses the body itself as a weapon. The dissemination of 'kamikazes', of men, boys, but women too, who kill themselves in order to kill other men and women, is a tragic phenomenon that unsettles and terrorizes the Western consciousness. No defence seems possible, except for more prevention-like obsessive surveillance, the militarization of the territory and the dissemination of suspicion and mistrust of whoever seems to have any possible connection with an Islamic fundamentalist, this too being a difficult quality to identify and distinguish from 'moderate' Islam.

Therefore, on the one hand, enemy bodies are invisible and can be annihilated from above with no risk of having to see them, or make them be seen. The first Gulf War, shown on TV, truly seemed nothing more than a video game which helped extinguish, in the West and above all in Europe, the horror of war that was still being fed by the memory of the devastations of World War II. 'They' perhaps die, but 'we' don't see them: 'we', instead, are untouchable, secure inside flying fortresses; because in reality, if whoever dies is not visible to whoever kills, the opposite is also true and perhaps more important: whoever kills is invisible, does not have a body, is, or is one with, a machine. Whoever kills must not die; their body must not be jeopardized and, when it happens that they are instead struck, this must be hidden from the view of their compatriots (this is in the US; in Italy it seems to be a different story).

Thus war re-enters the European and Western imagination as an event that is still possible, if not exactly normal. Conversely, enemy bodies that blow themselves up in order to kill us are an obscenity that is incomprehensible to 'us' and which contributes to radicalizing the perception of a distance, an almost anthropological difference between 'us' and 'them'. Yet here too, although in a backwards way, the body is, or is one with, a 'machine': the explosive, the airplane, the automobile carrying the explosives, etc. But if Westerners try to hide bodies, their own and those to be killed, 'others' exhibit them like a kind of last resort that is not only material but symbolic.

Preventive war, according to the US National Security Report,[1] is one of the options that is recognized and permitted by international law when there is a danger of an 'imminent threat', and consists of mobilizing troops on land, water and in the air that are prepared to attack. Nevertheless, today, the Report goes on, the situation has profoundly changed since the enemy is different than in the past. The enemy is global terrorism. And the strategy of deterrence that defeated the USSR does not work against global terrorism since the terrorist enemy is determined to destroy 'innocents', including by using 'so-called soldiers seeking to be martyrs through death, whose strongest defense is the fact that they are "not a state". We must adapt the concept of imminent threat to the capacities and objectives of today's adversaries: states and terrorists are not trying to attack us

---

1   See The White House (2002) The National Security Strategy of the United States of America, 2002. Available at http://www.whitehouse.gov/nsc/nss.html.

with conventional arms … they use acts of terror and, potentially, weapons of mass destruction – arms that are hidden and used without warning.'

Therefore, when necessary, there is a need to act by 'destroying the first threat that arrives at our borders'. The United States will not hesitate to act alone to defend itself by 'acting preventively against these terrorists, so they will not damage our people and our country'. After all, 'in the war against terrorism, we will never forget that we are ultimately fighting for our democratic way of life. Fear and freedom are at war, and there will be no fast or easy end to this conflict'.

Thus, the justification of preventive war, as a new strategy after the end of the Cold War and the fall of the USSR, makes use, on the one hand, of the formal recognition of the enemy's transformation: no more a powerful and very visible state. On the other hand and simultaneously, it makes use of the identification of this new, elusive and shifty enemy, to whom it is not even possible to grant the status of 'soldier', with 'rogue states', who are guilty not only of giving and providing aid and shelter to terrorists, but of amassing weapons of mass destruction, a move that in and of itself constitutes a serious threat to the United States, and which therefore justifies, even with respect to international law, a preventive war.

'Rogue states' are defined (The White House 2002) as follows:

> These states brutalize their very own people and deplete national resources for the personal gain of those governing; they show no respect whatsoever for international law, they threaten their neighbors and intentionally violate the international pacts they have signed; they are determined to acquire weapons of mass destruction, in addition to other advanced military instruments and to use them as a threat and offensively in order to attain the aggressive objectives of their regimes; they support global terrorism, and deny fundamental human values, and they hate the United States and everything that the United States symbolizes.

From this point of view, as many have noted, the US National Security Strategy tries to provide the justification for an infinite war, against an unspecified number of countries, in addition to the adoption of measures of intelligence, surveillance and restriction of civil rights both against 'foreigners' and against the residents and citizens of the United States itself. But what interests me here is the rhetorical use of the notion of 'prevention'. As in the case of crime, this use puts the US in the position of potential victim, and as in the case of security against the risk of becoming victims of crimes, in prevention against 'rogue' states there are a series of cumulative measures that range from help and assistance to the 'disadvantaged' to the surveillance of rogue states (the dangerous classes), the sterilization of the territory and, lastly, violent repression. Enemies are criminals and criminals are enemies. And crime and hostility are substantiated in the damage they cause or can cause to honest citizens, wherein they, in the case of the justification of war, identify themselves with the US and with 'everything that the US symbolizes', that is democracy, human values (significantly, not rights, but values, a much more imprecise and vague notion), the free market and so on. Emphasized among the measures of aid and assistance is indeed the opportunity of opening up the markets of poor countries to global exchange and strengthening and supporting the work of the World Bank and the International Monetary Fund. The autonomy and independence of these countries are desired just as in the case of individual citizens; but it is an autonomy and independence that is defined according to the cultural models and values of the democracy *par excellence*, the US. It is, therefore, an ability to do-it-yourself which means, on the one hand, not needing international aid but, on the other, conforming, both from an economic and a social and cultural point of view, to Western models.

Determining that a country has a hostile and threatening nature based on its hate of the United States is no small issue. They are (also) rogue because they bear sentiments of hatred against 'us'. It is not clear who is doing the hating (those governing or the people) and one question that is not asked is why 'we' are hated. Therefore, 'we' react to a feeling, a state of mind, before this is manifested in actions and beyond that manifestation.

Not asking why 'we' are hated is equivalent to believing this sentiment against 'us' entirely unreasonable, even irrational. This sentiment, then, cannot be based on anything but 'their' intrinsic malice, and this malice is indeed assigned, *de facto*, to their diversity compared to us, a diversity of 'values' and lifestyles: it is Samuel Huntington's *Clash of Civilizations*.

Naturally, a fundamental justification for preventive war is making it impossible for rogue states to use their weapons of mass destruction: in the US National Security Strategy, it is made clear that possessing or trying to possess weapons of mass destruction would render necessary a preventive armed intervention. It is therefore certain that such possession or attempt at possession is in and of itself a hostile act against the US, and metonymically, against Western civilization as a whole (democracy, freedom, etc.). It is too risky to allow states that are intrinsically barbaric and intrinsically geared towards the destruction of our civilization to be equipped with these weapons (while it is obvious, and even affirmed in the Report itself, that it is good and necessary that 'we' have them).

> Preventive war says: 'It is a dangerous world where many potential adversaries may be considering aggression against us or our friends, or may be acquiring the weapons that would allow them to do so, should they wish to: so we will declare war on that someone and interdict the possible unfolding of this perilous chain of could be's and would be's.' (Barber 2003: 108)

There is then here a notion of 'social dangerousness' that is entirely analogous to the one used for the internal enemy. It is in fact based on the characteristics of the 'perpetrator', who is imputed with intentions that are based actually on these characteristics, and it is the intentions that count in deciding whether to act preventively. In short, the risk represented by the fact that there are rogue states that equip themselves with weapons of mass destruction legitimizes preventive war.

In turn, the defining of rogue states – beyond the brutalization of those governing their own people, a brutality which, as is known, is also committed by states that are 'friends' of the United States, and therefore of 'Western civilization' – relies above all on the diversity of their 'values'.

And this diversity is affirmed, even inscribed, on bodies, for example in the torture rituals discovered in the Abu Ghraib jail. The female private dragging the prisoner around on a leash, a naked prisoner, is first of all certainly committing an act of extreme humiliation for men whose culture prescribes a maximum amount of modesty on the part of women, even the physical separation of women and men, the concealing of the body. Yet this ritual may also be interpreted as a way of affirming the extreme diversity and inferiority, compared to our own, of such cultural models: it indeed represents a female emancipation intended as assimilation of femininity by masculinity, absolute parity, to the point where it even turns into the humiliation and degradation of the 'different' male – the male who does not accept this parity. This parity is shown, exhibited, declared, as proof of the superiority of our civilization, and even, as in the case of the war in Afghanistan, as a principal motive for 'our' armed intervention (to free women from the burka). Western 'values' are not denied at Abu Ghraib, as many said after the discovery of the tortures. On the contrary, in a way, at least some of them are put on display and affirmed as superior, as indicative of a model civilization, in which men and women enjoy equal rights, wherein rights indicate, very reductively, the equal opportunity of treating others with cruelty.

The fact that preventive war does not help in combating terrorism or even in diminishing armed conflicts around the world, but is instead, as can be noted, used to increase and intensify their horror and violence, does not however mean that it does not have a symbolic efficacy. Yet this efficacy does not consist of producing a greater sense of security in those in the name of whose protection war is unleashed. It is doubtful, for example, that Americans now feel more secure, and in this case too we can note a resemblance with national and local security policies. As Barber notes (2003: 48–50), the measures that have been adopted up to this time against terror are multiplying terror itself:

> Terror succeeds in what it promises rather than in what it actually achieves, and so turns the effort against it into its chief tool. Code the danger levels! Arrest

every two-bit felon and call him a terrorist! Publicize vague threats! Label the war against it 'unending'! Bring down Saddam as a WMD addict, even if no weapons can be found! The terrorist can sit in a mountain cave or a Karachi slum and watch his enemies self-destruct around the initial fear he has seeded with a single and singular act of terror or with a few well-chosen follow-up threats that need not be made good on but which can be spread worldwide on a five-dollar tape ... Yet it is not terrorism but fear that is the enemy, and in the end fear will not defeat fear. Fear's empire leaves no room for democracy, while democracy refuses to make room for fear. In free societies, Franklin Roosevelt reminded us, 'The only thing we have to fear is fear itself' ... Preventive war will not in the end prevent terrorism; only preventive democracy can do that.

Nevertheless, this preventive war has the effectiveness that all wars and every identification of an enemy have: that of strengthening the collectivity of 'potential victims', the threatened collectivity, around a leader and a strategy that make broad use, in order to legitimize themselves, of the call to values indicated as at risk of erosion and crises, not only from the enemy, but also from internal fifth columns. In this sense, war is also preventive with respect to this risk: 'Christian values', 'family' and 'country' are at the core of the 'community' that many local security policies claim as, on the one hand, at risk, but on the other hand as the only possible contrast to 'crime' and disorder. Therefore trust is sought and found only in the particular, the personal, the familiar, the known, in tradition, in face-to-face relations. At the basis of this trust is similarity, as Durkheim (1989) recalls when speaking of 'simple' societies, and a consensus regarding the strong values that *de facto* consecrate the community itself.

Yet this means taking for granted and even welcoming the current crisis of institutions, their de-formalization, as well as the de-legitimization of law and rights in favour of a religious ethics. Institutions, as De Leonardis says (2001), are, in essence, what we have in common with respect to the bad, but also the good. They are the skeleton of a diversified and plural society that should 'hold out' thanks to a generalized trust of them, if they are neutral, impartial and authoritative (Offe 1999). They are, furthermore, what brings us together and draws us apart, or more accurately, what holds together different individuals, who are distinct from one another, singular, without making us get too close. They are also the vertical axis that gives profoundness and depth to social life, and creates a channel of communication between civil society and political power. Their crisis and de-formalization 'are freeing', yet at the same time they weaken and create a push towards seeking alliances in the similar, wiping out what, starting from our diversity, we have in common, and leaving a flat, horizontal society 'with exposed nerves' (De Leonardis 2001), for which the only way of communicating with power is through polls or revolt.

Prevention, Politics, Institutions, Law, Justice

If by politics we mean the active participation in creating a public discourse about the common good of people that are different from one another, that meet one another in a space which they have indeed constructed to be public, then the imperative to private and individualized prevention goes against this politics since it pushes each person to only take care of themselves and what belongs to them. And, as has been said, it is necessary to moreover take into account the tendency to produce enemies, to enclose oneself within communities of similar people, to sterilize and privatize public places, to 'de-corporalize', either through biological reductionism or through a push towards the virtual.

Without bodies, there is no diversity and there are no politics. There are no politics in the sense I noted before, and there is no public realm, if by that we mean a 'place' where it is possible to make visible what was previously private – in the sense of secret – making common what makes each and everybody different from all the others, including, indeed, the body as an unbreakable mix of nature and history, product and producer of relations.

Naturally, in turn, private and individualized prevention *is* a politics, a method of managing power and, as has been seen, a method for producing and exercising social control. It is a politics that makes use of the 'capital of fear' (as Bauman 2005 calls it) and which is exercised through the push towards isolation and separation. This, by no coincidence, corresponds to the tendency to construct charismatic leaders that present themselves without further mediations as the point of reference of a 'people' comprised of individuals, each one having no significant relations with the others.

'Light' and fluid institutions are adequate for an individual liberty which in reality is revealed as constant censure and self-control and which at the same time pushes towards seeking refuge in new or rediscovered certainties: in addition to family, as traditionally understood, religions and ethnic groups, which appeal to family, and, as a hinge and symbol of it, women and their bodies. Women are indeed, even in our societies, the object of a renewed attack, which is directed against certain hard-won freedoms, and which first of all concern the availability of one's own body and its procreative abilities.

The law *par excellence* of societies with weak and fluid institutions is contract law. The logic of contract tends to extend all the way down, from economic transactions to relations between individuals to national and local public policies (through the various forms of partnerships with companies, volunteer work, the third sector) and the contract is one of the principle methods for 'carrying out prevention' within the national states, whether it is purchased (insurance policies, private security companies, alarm systems, etc.) or negotiated on between public entities and private companies.

We talk moreover of *lex mercatoria* to indicate the prevailing method of legal normativity of the globalized word, the source of which is major law firms, in particular American firms; it is a law consisting of norms that regulate commercial exchanges and the relations between corporations. This is private law, just as private law comprises the norms resulting from arbitrators' decisions.[2]

Case law, including the case law of international courts, like the courts of Luxembourg and Strasburg, is also obviously indicative of this fluidity and flexibility.

And yet, prevention also has another dimension – much more consistent and tough – which makes use of the construction of new institutions, in addition to the attempt to strengthen old ones. This occurs within and by national states, but also through and by means of agreements between them. The other side of fluidity and flexibility is indeed repression and control through instruments that often lie outside the law and are detrimental to rights: war, and along with this the administrative expulsions of non-citizens, the temporary residence centres for 'illegals' and those seeking asylum, and all the measures adopted to face an increasingly threatening, insidious and elusive terrorism (the extension of police checkpoints, collection of data via the Internet and email, the use and abuse of wire tapping, and so on).

Here returns the body: containment and exclusion are directed at bodies, at people who are identified through their corporeity, whereas rights and law seem instead to count for those who can de-corporalize themselves or who are viewed as de-corporalized. Temporary residence centres are illuminating examples of this.

Rights have become another one of the normative languages that prevail today. Through this language, justice can be obtained not only within one's own national state, but elsewhere as well by turning to any one of the international courts. Rights travel, or should travel, with people. Yet they have become a language that lends itself to many uses, even contrasting ones, as in the justification of wars, for example, including preventive war. In short, it appears that rights are used much more as a rhetoric, or better yet, perhaps, as a call to a morality that wants to be universal, rather than as juridical principles, and therefore legal constraints (Pitch 2004).

This rhetoric of rights seems to go along well with a way of conceiving freedom as inherent to an individual who does not have connections and relations,

---

2   A special issue of the journal *Sociologia del diritto* [Sociology of Law], XXXII, 2005 No. 2–3, is entirely dedicated to *lex mercatoria*.

all the more so because the ones that are continuously evoked are civil rights, while social rights are muted. Furthermore, it is a rhetoric that separates 'our' rights from those of 'others', calling the latter *human* rights and intending them, *de facto*, to be the minimum rights for the survival of whoever does not have and cannot have anything else, whereas 'ours' are instead declaimed as articulate and complex rights: the (individual) right to 'security' is, for example, one of the rights that is often so called.

The rights to security and civil liberties obviously contrast with one another and as has been seen it is security that prevails for all. It prevails, though, to the point of entirely deferring liberties, above all for the 'others', those 'others' who are already in our country, those 'others' who arrive here or would like to do so, and many of the 'others' who are in their own countries. The prevention of terrorism, security understood as the protection from violence and illegality, simultaneously brings with it a call to the rhetoric of rights and the violation of rights themselves. Protected rights, then, end up being those for the freedom of circulation of goods and of people belonging to the wealthy elite. In this sense, it is true that rights are the legal form that is most adapted to globalization (Ferrarese 2002), a method of mediation and communication that passes through, on the one side, contractualization, and on the other side, the Westernization of the world.

Without institutions that guarantee them however, rights too are flexible, even fluctuating, and lend themselves to every use, ultimately becoming either pure rhetoric or a vocabulary to justify almost everything, including many atrocities. In this context, one should ask oneself if it is true, as the legal realists maintain, that the only 'true' rights, that is those that are protected, exercisable, are those guaranteed by the constitutions of national states, and that it is the modern nation state alone that is not just, *de facto*, but can, even prospectively, become equipped for this purpose.[3] Not a new thesis, of course, as Hannah Arendt (1951) has already stated it, in relation to the status of refugees and stateless people.

It is not an objective of this book to discuss this problem. Yet it is impossible not to recall, along with the now extremely extensive literature regarding problems of the internationalization of rights, and regarding so-called multiculturalism, the arguments proposed by, among others, Appadurai (2005), according to whom minorities and majorities are born together, and it is precisely *also* through a rhetoric and a policy of rights that they pass from procedural to substantial, producing *cultural* differences which in turn are one of the roots of contemporary violence.

---

3   However, see Rodotà (2006) who, in talking about a growing 'tourism of rights', brings to light the possibility of a universalization 'from below'.

But the suspension of rights is exactly what constitutes one of the truly hard institutions of today, the temporary residence centres established in Europe, and not just the Europe of the Schengen Treaty, to contain the migrants and refugees of the southern world. These centres, in turn, refer back to other similar institutions, Guantanamo for example, and Abu Ghraib prison, but also, more pertinently, to the islands where Australia sends its migrants (Perera 2006); and, recently, the camps established in Libya with the collaboration of Italy and Germany to detain or send back migrants. All of these institutions bring to mind refugee camps which were set up under emergency circumstances and then became permanent, which is especially true in the case of the Palestinian camps.

What they have in common is the construction of a space outside the law and outside of rights, a kind of limbo where people without a defined status are enclosed, or to put it more accurately, a space that defines the people who are enclosed as non-persons (Dal Lago 1999). This demonstrates how globalization has immeasurably increased the number of these non-persons, precisely because, at least for the poor, those coming from the southern world and so on, globalization did not entail the disappearance or even the attenuation of the boundaries of national states, the only body that grants and recognizes legal, and furthermore social, citizenship. The people confined in these institutions are in fact not holders of any right, but at most the object of charity and assistance, on which, it remains to be said, many NGOs live and prosper.

In the name of prevention, security from the risk of crime, illegality and, above all, currently, terrorism, boundaries are secured and the law suspended. For this purpose as well, it is appropriate to cite Barber (2003: 111–112):

> The same logic of exceptional circumstances, novel adversaries, and altered technology is used to rationalize preventive detention. As Joseph Lelyveld articulates the argument (on the way to criticizing it): 'Jihadists are different from other Warriors, in that their struggles won't obviously be ended by an armistice or surrender proclaimed on high. The overriding objective of any detention regime in these circumstances has to be the gathering of intelligence about the network and its targets that may serve to prevent attacks. Prevention is more important than prosecuting individuals for past actions. If you are looking to the future, it's hard to say who among the detainees is important – that is, dangerous – and who's not.'

The inclusion/exclusion dynamic, typical of the modern state, becomes consolidated by extending worldwide and producing more and more 'wasted lives' (Bauman 2004).

The Exception and the Rule

Camps, as Agamben (1995) notes, are a modern invention, and one that has been central in establishing politics in modernity. The camp is at once law and non-law, lying in an indeterminate zone between inclusion and exclusion, and whoever is enclosed there is the new *homo sacer*, killable and unsacrificable, what Agamben himself calls the 'naked life'.[4]

The literature on camps is now very extensive. In *The Origins of Totalitarianism*, Arendt (1951) was the first to indicate their significance in modern politics and to point out how they showed the defeat of 'human' rights, insofar as the 'naked' humanity there enclosed – precisely those for whom rights were supposed to be for – was totally deprived of them, revealing how indeed it's only the rights of citizens and not those of 'men' that can be exercised. Camps date back to colonial times; the first camps, intended to enclose entire populations, were the Cuban *campos de concentraciónes* (first established in 1896) where the colonizers enclosed colonized insurgents (see Nuzzo 2008, and the literature therein cited).

It is the experience of colonialism that comes to be translated into the culture and practice of eliminating, in the etymological sense of 'pushing to the limits', those who do not belong to the nation, and cannot or are constructed as not being able to acquire the characteristics of 'citizens'.

The state of exception, according to Agamben (2003), has now been extended, and what was once considered exceptional is now considered normal. We live in an oxymoron, a state of permanent exception; it's an oxymoron which is moreover analogous to calling migrant camps temporary residence centres.

As concerns the condition of refugees and those seeking asylum, Bauman (2004: 76), citing Michel Agier, says that they are *'hors du nomos* – outside of the law; not this law or that law of this or that country, *but law as such*. They are outcasts and outlaws of a novel kind, the products of globalization and the fullest epitome and incarnation of its frontierland spirit.' And indeed:

> as globalization takes its toll, new camps … mushroom around the spots of conflagration, prefiguring the model Tony Blair wishes the UN High Commission for refugees to render obligatory. For instance, the three camps of Dabaab, populated by as many people as the rest of the Kenyan Garissa province in which they were located in 1991–2, show no signs of imminent closure, yet till this very day they do not appear on the map of the country. (ibid. 76)

---

4   Life, naturally, is never naked. Feminism – and psychoanalysis – have well demonstrated how it is always 'dressed' in language, in words. Nevertheless, it can be construed and managed as 'naked', which is precisely what occurs in the case of camps.

To that end, it's worth reiterating Bauman's (2004) reflection on waste, which is no longer recyclable and not even able to be relegated elsewhere, since elsewhere no longer exists. It's waste that is also, and even above all, *human* waste, to be hidden from view and somehow made inoffensive. Yet as human refugees multiply, so does waste multiply – temporary residence centres, refugee camps – and along with it the protected and supervised places that keep out the dangers that are traceable to the waste itself. Order, which has always produced its exclusions, thus at once expands and contracts: it expands because it seeks to extend to the entire globe; it contracts because there is no longer an elsewhere to unload the waste, which is in turn multiplying, due to this very attempt at expansion.

Conclusions

In this section, I'll return to the questions raised in the Introduction.

A society of prevention is a society that lives, although in the present, in a present that is projected towards a future that it perceives as threatening, heralding dangers, rather than promises of a better life.

A society where the imperative to prevention is individualized and privatized is a society in which even many of the practices of social control tend to become private, to be demanded from the market (surveillance, private police forces, security contracts, the use of electronic identification devices). However, the synergies between public and private do not refer back to the panoptic figure, a metaphor that is too centralized to symbolize the current attitude of social control, nor do they refer to a Big Brother. Insofar as our personal data circulate from one database to another, there is no one single collector; indeed sometimes information being too available creates nothing but deafening noise and confusion.

Still, naturally, the perception of the possibility of being monitored incessantly, whether this monitoring is real or not, is already a powerful method of social control (and here, the function of the hidden controller in the panoptic tower, invisible to the eyes of those controlled, is pertinent: the controller may or may not be there, but what counts is that whoever is being controlled can't know, and must behave as if the controller is always there).

Yet, as Lyon and Rodotà note, many of today's devices of control are much more impersonal: they are directed at us, they channel us through instruments that we ourselves want to use, since they simplify life for us (credit cards, bar codes, the insertion of electronic chips under the skin to facilitate our identification and visibility, and so on). At the same time, as has been shown, these devices function to produce a trust that is otherwise non-existent or insufficient. In doing so, they thus discriminate against and exclude entire classes of the population to whom these devices are not granted, and who are therefore not considered worthy of preliminary trust. Thus these same 'dangerous people', these classes, are subject to a much less impersonal control, which is much more explicitly repressive, even entailing imprisonment (as well as, naturally, exclusion from all of the property, resources and places for which the above devices are necessary). Along with the widespread, impersonal control that we ourselves implement as a method of exercising 'freedom', which is in fact closely intertwined with this, the pressure towards individual prevention refers to an imperative that drips with moral values: responsibility, autonomy, independence.

The imperative of prevention thus takes two directions, as I have said numerous times: on the one hand it privatizes and individualizes, on the other hand it becomes a reality in institutions that are not at all fluid and permeable. Social control both makes and makes use of moralizing calls to assuming individual responsibility and impersonal and 'actuarial' methods.

The duo of prevention–security, wherein security is defined as personal safety, reveals how central fear is in our societies. It also reveals how it can be used to produce a social order, however precarious, that can do without horizontal and vertical solidarity and intense social ties. In such an order, governance is instead based on the continuous creation of dangers and enemies, separating us, pushing each person to only trust in those who are similar to them, and even more so in their own family members, thus creating a territorial distance between the bearers of other cultures, segregating and excluding those who cannot take care of themselves.

Women are central in this order, both materially and symbolically. Individualized and privatized prevention does not only correspond to one's increased self-control (and often self-censure), but becomes a primary duty of care work, multiplying the tasks and responsibilities towards children, the infirm, the elderly, but adult males too.

Also, from a symbolic point of view, control of women and their bodies is at the basis of any call for the strengthening and production of old and new communities, whether invented or 'rediscovered'. Women's freedoms are one of the ingredients of fear, of widespread contemporary insecurity; the old ghosts of disorder and chaos accumulate on them, and are today renewed by technologies that are perceived as devices that enable women to hold nature in check, to become the masters of life (and therefore of death). Many calls to the 'laws of nature', as supreme regulators of life (many new prohibitions are legitimated and justified by the superior necessity to respect 'nature' – an Italian example of this is Law 40 on assisted procreation) threaten not only women's freedoms, but their health too. They have the precise sense of imposing a control and domination over women, deemed necessary for the purpose of containing fear.

Precariousness, forced nomadism, the fragility of identity boundaries, scientific innovations and technologies, which upset the meaning of life and death, produce an anthropology of fear that places on women and their bodies the ultimate responsibility for keeping such fear in check, for reproducing a familiar symbolic and material order, a traditional common sense. Identity is sought in tradition, that is in something that has always referred to both nature and the norm, to those values and absolute thruths which are indeed supposed to be spelt out by nature and religion. Nature and religion, on the other hand, have often been made to coincide with women and their bodies. As a result of this, women and their bodies must remain under male domination (by virtue of nature, norm, religion).

Nor does war, preventive or otherwise, escape this paradigm. The justifications for the recent asymmetrical wars made extensive use of the theme of the 'defence of women', where women's rights and freedoms, claimed to be unacknowledged and violated by the enemies, thus pronounced 'barbaric', uncivilized, were frequently cited. This conceals not just the old justifications for colonial domination but, above all, the traditional representation of men as saviours and protectors of women, who are thus reduced to the rank of minors, objects of benevolence, rather than being recognized as individuals, persons in their own right. It is no coincidence that during the war in Afghanistan to 'free women from the burka', the voices of Afghan women's organizations were silenced and ignored, and the women themselves and their rights forgotten after the (very temporary) defeat of the Taliban. As for the new wars described by Mary Kaldor (2006), the affirmation of a more or less reinvented identity has made ample use of the practice of so-called 'ethnic rape', a central practice of 'ethnic cleansing'.

But there are other aspects of prevention that must be examined from a gendered viewpoint. The obsession with security, both at the national level and above all at the local level (which is fundamental since it is at this level that, as we saw, various kinds of experiments and projects of prevention are concentrated) appeals on the one hand to fears which are very often defined as being feminine, or which adopt a rhetoric that was once used for women and minors (victimization). On the other hand, it does not at all take into account how women and men experience the city differently, and it fails to address the security of more than half of the population: women.

I said some time ago that the only city that would be safe for women would be one without men (Pitch and Ventimiglia 2001). That's a paradox, obviously, but it illustrates a fact that has mainly been ignored by local security policies: that is, that dangers are sexed as male, for women and men, and that a sterilization of the 'public' territory has little to offer women, who are much more likely to be threatened by acquaintances, family members, friends, parents, within the walls of the house, at work or at school, than on some dark corner in the city. And yet, as noted, the imperative to individual prevention is a powerful method of censure and self-censure for women, operating as a prohibition against freely using the city and its opportunities and resources, which means the world and its resources.

The obsession with security, and therefore with prevention, pervades institutional policies and tends to heavily affect a politics intended as participation in the definition and management of the common good, not just through the restriction of the public realm, but also through the push towards taking care of only oneself and construing the other as a possible enemy. Women's politics, a politics that is nurtured by relations, particularly suffers from this and, once again, what becomes constrained is the freedom that is connected to such a policy (Boccia 2003; Pitch 2004b).

Freely playing with identities, fragmenting them and pluralizing them, as it is being asked by those who welcome the possibility of liberation *from* bodies, in particular for women, who through and because of their bodies undergo an added domination, is possible for only very few men and women (not unlike the freedom to travel the globe), and does not avoid discriminations and inequalities, does not put 'normality' in check, but simply condemns diversity (from the 'normality') inscribed in bodies to the point of concealment and exclusion, and reinforces for many men (and, alas, many women) the push towards an essentialized and substantialized identity. Furthermore, as I already noted, the disappearance of bodies, which are, at the same time, nature and culture, contributes to impoverishing the public realm, even definitively emptying it, and in this way deprives politics of its sense and meaningfulness.

As for institutions, the viewpoint of prevention shows that, if it is true that many of them have become fragile, not very regulative, permeable – and therefore incapable, in bad but also good circumstances, of containing us, guiding us and showing us what we have in common – others, on the other hand, have become strong, hard places where rights are ignored and the paradigm of the camps is repeated, used to exclude, even to define who ends up there as non-persons, waste, rejects. Law and rights are luxuries for this population; even criminal law, even penalties, prison, insofar as today they are explicitly called upon to contain and neutralize, incapacitate rather than 'rehabilitate', and are used against those who are identified as the bearers of a particular identity rather than against those who have committed a crime, prove to be a privilege to someone confined in Guantanamo, or at some temporary residence centre.

Risk and prevention refer back to an uncertainty and insecurity that today go beyond what was inscribed in the first, solid modernity. Nevertheless, it may very well be that, perhaps not in the West, or at least not by us Westerners, they (the uncertainty and insecurity) might now produce, even more than in the first modernity (the world having expanded, and the method of perceiving and managing insecurity and uncertainty having become diversified and pluralized), a push towards still unimagined novelties. From this point of view, as Rodotà (2006) appropriately notes, tourism of rights which here can produce a new citizenship based on one's financial means,[5] might instead be heralding a universalization of these very rights from the bottom up. Residents of the southern world, migrants, refugees, those seeking asylum, could be, together with women, who are always an integral and active part of these groups, in the *avant garde* of a new composite and plural 'civilization', equipped as they are with the past and their bodies, and projected towards the future in a way in which we (well, we, in the sense of *men*, males, from the northern world, etc.) do not seem to be anymore. But that, obviously, is another story.

---

5   An Italian example of this is the use by many women and couples of Swiss, Spanish and other assisted procreation centres in order to escape the prohibitions of Law 40. Conversely, there is the acceptance of requests for political asylum from women who want to escape genital mutilation.

Epilogue

Since I wrote this book, much seems to have changed. The international financial and economic crisis has brought the state back into the economic scene, neoliberal rhetoric and policies appear for what they are: a recipe for disaster, Obama's election to the US presidency has wiped out the call for and justification of 'preventive wars', but even more importantly his victory has brought back a sense of hope in the future.

Actually, though, the even greater scarcity of resources might instead lead to a more intense struggle of everybody against each other. In Italy, alas, this seems to be the case, judging from the measures this government has launched against migrants, the homeless, gypsies, and the dismal common sense such measures produce and support.

And how we come out of this crisis depends on *how* the state will come back onto the scene, to the support of what and whom, and with what legitimacy and consensus. The state is not synonymous with the public, and the public, in turn, is not necessarily the same as shared, participated, solidary action. Neoliberal rhetoric may be discredited, but this does not mean that it will be easy for states to re-regulate financial and other markets. Also, of course, in a time of scarce resources it is improbable that much public money will be given to finance social and health services.

From my (albeit restricted and 'provincial') Italian location, I observe two contradictory sentiments, as they may be read through the media, the web and blogs included. On the one hand, the enthusiasm with which many people saluted Obama's election (hope in a new future), on the other hand the impotence these same people express at what they themselves can actually do to change things in Italy (pessimism for one's own present). Also, there are many others, our government, as I said, included, whose reaction to the financial crisis takes the form of a renewed fear and diffidence towards migrants, and in general everybody who is not 'us'. Calls for community sentiments reinforce blood and soil rhetoric, the search for a 'true Italian' identity, and eventually result in racist attacks, which are unfortunately on the increase. Thus, prevention rhetoric tends to be increasingly used to legitimate repressive national and local penal and security policies, while the command to be self-reliant is supported by the incitation to be thrifty and ready for sacrifices.

It is mainly women who face the burden of thriftiness, and in general of care for the family such as to withstand the crisis.

In Italy we do appear 'special': explicitly racist ministers, a conflict of interest of unheard of magnitude in the so-called liberal democracies of the West, a prime minister apparently intent in showing to the rest of the world that we've finally entered a post-feminist era. But are we Italians really so special? Though of course here everything is taken to its dangerous – and ridiculous – extremes, one may ask if what's happening in Italy is unique, or if, instead, it says something important about the state of our democracies.

Rather than approaching these questions directly, I shall discuss two books published after I wrote mine, as many of the issues presented here are analysed there, but with different conclusions. They discuss in much greater depth than I have done here two aspects I have linked under the label of prevention: Jonathan Simon (2007) takes on the issue of how fear is at the bottom of a type of government widespread in the US (at least before Obama), while Nicholas Rose (2007) examines the paradigm of self and government emerging from molecular biology and genetics.

I actually think that my being situated in a part of the Western world which rarely appears in analyses written in English might offer a novel point of view. Writing from the margins is both a disadvantage and a potential advantage, as feminism (among other things) has demonstrated. Also, we are too often in the habit of assuming that what happens in the English-speaking world merely anticipates processes which, in time, will spread everywhere. That may be true, but apart from the fact that these processes will probably change and have different consequences in different parts of (our) world, it might also be that a view from the margins might shed a different light on these same processes and/or that, on the other hand, it is precisely what happens at the margins that could spread elsewhere (it did happen with fascism, after all).

I think that, for example, the grotesque way in which sex and gender are being played out on the contemporary Italian political scene does not spell our 'backwardness', nor our not having had a strong and vocal feminist movement, but quite the opposite. I mean to say that the new freedoms won by women in the 1970s and 1980s of the last century have spurred an often violent reaction, tinged by fear: traditional patriarchy has not been replaced by a 'new' masculinity, leaving many men in a sort of 'anomic' situation, which in Italy has led to an increase of violence by partners and ex-partners, and to the insistent attempt at reducing women, yet again, to bodies without voice. If that is true, one could learn something from our present vicissitudes that could shed some light on gender and sexual relationships in liberal democracies today. The same might hold true for issues related to security, social control and, of course, prevention. At least, I hope so.

Nicholas Rose's book explores the emergence of a new type of biopower and biopolitics based on current trends in biology and genomics. Within the ethos of advanced liberal democracies – an ethos mandating autonomy, individual freedom, prudence and self-responsibility – the shift to molecular biology and molecular genomics, supports significant changes in the technologies of self. The emergence of a new somatic and biological citizenship is the result – and summary – of such changes.

Contrary to many critics who impute to the new discoveries and new technologies in this field a novel type of biological determinism, Rose attempts to show how this 'biological citizen' is indeed a very active one, while his freedom is enhanced by the enormously extended opportunities to choose and shape her and her progenies' future. All this, he maintains, is within a new 'economy of hope' produced by the diverse and varied hopes of different actors (patients or prospective patients and their 'genetic' family and lineages; novel communities gathering around a specific health issue; doctors; researchers; pharmaceutical companies, etc.).

While health and body have been at the centre of political preoccupations and power techniques for at least over two centuries, Rose indicates two fundamental transformations: the first has to do with the uncoupling of the link nation (and population)-territory under the control of the state; which means, he says, new configurations for 'populations' and the entering onto the scene of a multitude of private or semi-private actors dealing with health and bodies together with the national state.

The second has to do with the emergence of molecular biology and genomics, which have introduced a new style of thought and engineered an individualized and privatized 'politics of life'. Molecular biology promises to produce a predictive, preventive and personalized medicine, consistent with the requirement, increasingly intended in biological and somatic terms, that the new biological citizen be an accurate and prudent strategist and designer of his life. Being and remaining healthy is a fundamental moral imperative in our societies, and it means maximizing for oneself and others the living body's potentialities. Indeed, Rose says, the borders between therapy, correction and maximization have dissolved so that today a good quality of life entails for the individual not just a careful, positive and informed style of life, and the search for the appropriate therapy for already visible pathological symptoms, but also, and fundamentally, availing herself of those genetic tests capable to predict one's 'susceptibility' to the development of future pathologies, plus doing all that is possible to increase one's physical and mental 'potentialities', and searching on the market for the proper pharmaceutical drugs. Thus, the good life shifts from the level of *bios* to that of *zoe*, that is to our somatic (and 'animal') self. There is, Rose contends, a 'somatization of ethics', whereby we relate to ourselves as 'biological' beings, and the good citizen is the one who takes maximum care of her health and bodily potentialities.

Contrary to old-style genetic research, and therefore testing, molecular genomics is more complex, adopts a probabilistic posture, and, as it does not anymore look for the single gene 'responsible for', takes into consideration environmental and other factors whose interaction might produce a particular result. We are then confronting an extremely individualized medicine which calls for an extremely individualized prevention. At the same time, Rose points to the emergence and growth of new communities, where individuals suffering from a particular pathology, or knowing to be susceptible to the development of a future pathology, discuss, analyse, gather information, put pressure on public and private research institutions – in a word are active participants in this new 'economy of hope'.

Rose takes on the critics of genetic screening and testing, first of all showing the difference with past eugenic practices, then refuting the accusations of biological reductionism and determinism (biology is no longer destiny) by showing the role of individual responsibilities in choices and decisions regarding oneself. The state is not the only one, nor the decisive actor, in promoting and dispensing resources for the well-being of its citizens: at most, its role is one of facilitator, coherently with the more general changes in its functions.

Many of the characteristics he imputes to the present social and political scenario are the same as the ones I also indicate: the attempt at harnessing the future, the shift towards an individualized and privatized prevention, the centrality and ethical character of the call to prevention in contemporary biopolitics, and the importance of this command for individual responsibility. Yet, his conclusions are quite different.

I think that this difference has to do with two aspects: first, he is less interested in the effects of social control of these characteristics than I am; secondly, he interprets these same effects in a Foucaultian key, e.g., as a new instance of the same type of subjectivization Foucault registered in first modernity. For Foucault, the internalization of discipline is the very substance of individual freedom. What is new today, with the emergence of a biopower based on molecular biology, is that this subjectivity is a somatic and biological one, so that citizenship is also biological and somatic. Just as Foucault, however, Rose does not acknowledge any difference between female and male subjectivization.

Rose notes the demise of the third dimension, the loss of profundity and the domination of flatness, both in the perception of self and in that of the world, but he doesn't perceive this as a problem for political agency.

The importance of the body – in somatic and biological terms – the possibility to change it at will, the reduction of the mind to the workings of the brain – also to be played at will via drugs obtainable on the market – spells an era, Rose appears to say, when we must at the same time revaluate the Cartesian mind–body dichotomy and salute the feminist call to make 'our bodies our own, and ourselves'.

Here, I think, is the point where we diverge most. Rose's analysis does not take gender and sexual difference into account, whereas the changes he describes have a differential impact according to them (and race and social status, but these he acknowledges, at least to a point). More importantly, feminist thought and experience interpret the body as the site of self in quite a different way from Rose, and, of course, Cartesio and his late readers. In turn, this leads to a totally different manner of conceiving freedom and political agency. I shall return to these issues after discussing Jonathan Simon's book.

With Simon, we go from biological citizen to victim of crime. Indeed, Simon affirms that nowadays, at least in the US, the paradigm of the 'good citizen' is the victim of crime. This is due to the style of government which has been replacing the welfare compromise of the New Deal since the early 1970s of the last century. Governing through crime, according to Simon, has become the paradigm of governance, not just for criminal justice, but for all the institutions of contemporary America, from the family to schools. Crime, and the fear of crime, suggest, support and justify the great internment which sees a disproportionate percentage of the US population (especially black and Latino males) under custody, but they also are at the core of provisions limiting the freedom of the middle classes. These last, in order to defend themselves, shut themselves within gated communities and/or sponsor and require the diffusion of CCTV and other similar gadgets.

Simon's analysis, according to De Giorgi (2008), at the same time adds and distances itself both from cultural analyses and structural analyses of contemporary social control. The first, imputed to David Garland, describes a 'culture of control' where crime is simultaneously constructed as a routine event of everyday life and produced by 'aliens', those dangerous and undesirable 'others' to be neutralized. In Garland's view, the crime as a 'routine event … inspires situational prevention policies, devoid of claims to values, which produce an 'order' in contradiction with the old ideals of moral discipline and obedience to authority, but in line with neoliberal attempts at a 'lighter' state.

The construct of crime as a product of 'dangerous others', on the other hand, appears to contrast with neoliberal ethos as well as with old welfare ideals. This construct promotes vengeance, the defence of society and the neutralization of evil, consistent with neoconservative values. It is this last construct that is at the basis of the US great internment of recent decades. But, according to Garland, between the neoliberal ideology of free market and neoconservative and populist authoritarianism there is constant tension so that it is not possible to draw a causal link between neocapitalist restructuring and the changes in the control culture.

Which is what Wacquant (1999) does. In his view, we are in the presence of a penal state replacing the welfare state, totally in line with the neoliberal project of deregulating and thinning the public sector. The penal state, Wacquant maintains, represents the other side of this project, as it expresses a politics that criminalizes poverty. Such politics, he says, are functional to the imposition of underpaid and precarious labour conditions and to the contemporary reformulation of social policies in punitive terms.

Simon retrodates the discursive processes which introduced the new governance paradigm he describes to the legitimacy crisis of the New Deal which started from Barry Goldwater's 1964 election campaign. The language of law and order, the periodic calls to 'war' (on crime, drugs, poverty, terrorism) shape a governance paradigm based on the prevention and neutralization of risks which pervades all institutional contexts. This distances his analysis from a purely 'vertical' (De Giorgi 2008: XXIV) explanation, such as that of Wacquant, and allows him to both describe the political institutional changes and those happening in the styles of life, work and consumption in a less, so to speak, haphazard way than Garland.

As I think is clear from the preceding pages, I too think that there is no contradiction between neoliberalism and authoritarian populism. Indeed, contemporary Italy is an extreme example of a country with both, at least on the discursive level.

But what I want to take on here is Simon's contention that the victim of crime is nowadays the paradigm of the 'good' (and real) citizen. As early as 1989 (Pitch 1989, 1995) I wrote as much, but I reached this conclusion via a relatively different path: I analysed the women's movement campaign for a new rape law and I noticed the discursive shift from casting themselves as oppressed to presenting themselves as victims – a significant shift, not just for the women's movement. It signalled, I wrote, the re-emergence on the public and political scene of actors, who until then, at least in Italy, had been hidden within references to 'the system', 'historical processes', etc.

But what kind of actors were they? The use of the symbolic potential of the criminal justice system meant the return on the scene of de-contextualized actors, devoid of any characteristic apart from having suffered a crime. Such a move, on the part of the women's movement, was geared to establish the innocence of rape victims, at the cost, however, of radically simplifying heterosexual relationships, and of conferring voice on the basis of victimization. That move, new in the Italian political context, characterized until then by reference to 'classes' and 'oppression', was taken up by other groups, namely the 'victims of terrorism', 'mafia', relatives of mentally ill people, etc. In a word, being or calling oneself a victim became the basis for voice and political agency. A political agency, however, limited to single issues and to the time necessary to put them on the political agenda. Nimby activities, to stop gypsies camping in the neighbourhood, or prostitutes practising in nearby streets, or, more recently, against immigrants, follow from this pattern. What I think should also be noted is the feminization of contemporary political agency. Victim is a label which establishes the innocence of those who use it for themselves, but also their vulnerability, their (relative) weakness, their being in the position traditionally imputed to women, children, the old.

Is there a relationship, and of what kind, between the biological citizen and the victim of crime? Well, it is precisely their vulnerability. Rose calls it, in medical terms, susceptibility – to the development of certain diseases. But whereas Simon sees the centrality of the victim of crime in political discourse and policies as a threat to democracy, Rose situates the biological citizen within a new economy of hope.

Simon draws a scenario governed by fear and vengeance, Rose by hope in the future. Both, however, describe an extremely individualized and insecure 'society' where political agency is punctual, issue-oriented, and, in Simon's case, defensive. Neither adopts a gendered view.

As they look at different aspects of contemporary society and use different material, their differences may be considered obvious. Yet, both use a Foucaultian lens, and both are interested in the interaction between policies of social control and contemporary subjectivity.

In this book I have tried a comprehensive overview, linking issues like criminal justice and contemporary medicine under the imperative of prevention. In my conclusions I talked of an anthropology of fear and of the centrality of women in this anthropology. I contended that identity is searched for in what stands for nature, and that nature is equated with the norm, e.g., normality, and both together mean 'tradition and male domination'. Moreover, contrary to what Rose appears to say, I interpret the moral imperative to preventing illnesses and intervening on one's bodies and minds, all the way down to genes, in order to fulfil it, not in terms of more freedom, but instead in terms of constant self-discipline, self-censorship. And I see the subjectivity arising from this as an empty one, incapable of effective political agency, which I impute to incarnated selves, something completely different from Rose's biological citizens.

Our Bodies Ourselves, the title of a famous feminist book of the 1970s, expresses a view opposite to the Cartesian one, contrary to what Rose thinks about the book's view. The book, and the rallying cry that was taken from its title, wanted to signify the inextricable unity of body and mind, to the point where the mind was supposed to be 'sexed' (gendered) because of a sexed body. The mind is, in *Our Bodies Ourselves*, seen not as sovereign and master of the body. The present image of the mind as the working brain, analysed in its smallest components and linkages, does embody the mind, but curiously, in Rose's analysis, it is a mind that still controls and distances itself from the body, insofar as it is the protagonist of decisions to intervene on the body, brain included. Thus, it is a sovereign brain/mind and indeed Rose favourably quotes Hacking's saying that we ought to go back to Cartesio.

Feminism has long discussed the body and its role in individual subjectivity. There are many and diverse views, but not concerning intrinsic unity of body and mind. Rather, discussion has centred on the nature–culture relationship, whether gender is a social construct imposed on a biological (natural) being or whether there is no way to distinguish nature and culture, insofar as what we call nature is always already a cultural construct. However, this discussion shows not only that feminism reclaims the unity of mind and body, but also that it endorses a 'heavy' image of the body, one that sees the body as inextricably nature and culture, biology and history.

Yet, the women's movement's campaign for new rape laws was certainly an important factor in legitimating the 'victim of crime' as a fundamental political subject, and, eventually, the 'good' and true citizen. This has happened in Italy, but the shift to 'realist' left criminology of former radical British criminologists in the early 1980s testifies to the impulse the women's movement also gave to this elsewhere. The use of the symbolic potential of penality spread in the 1980s: campaigns against child abuse, against sexual harassment, against mobbing, etc. They all used the discourse and logic of the penal system, whatever they actually asked for. That this happened, at least in Italy, on the part of political actors, who were until then strongly against the actual functioning of the criminal justice system, helped in reconstructing the political scenario around single-issue battles. It also simplified the actors themselves, legitimating their 'voice' on the basis of having suffered or potentially being in the condition of suffering from a single problem.

As I said, the criminal justice system produces decontextualized actors, whose only relevant characteristic is the capacity to 'understand and want' (as the Italian penal law states). Because, indeed, one of the main objectives of these campaigns, the women movement's included, was not just to reconstruct themselves as political actors, but also to impute responsibility for their problems to well-identified individuals, the innocence of victims is strictly related to the intentional wrongdoing of perpetrators, who are to be held responsible regardless of social context or relationships with victims.

Individual responsibility gets centre stage, after decades of imputing responsibilities to 'society', 'capitalism', the 'system', even 'patriarchy'. Thus, the simplification and individualization of actors is not the product solely of neoliberal thinking and neoliberal policies. And these same thinking and policies make abundant use of the discourse and logic of the criminal justice system.

Of course, we might lead all this under the label 'structural changes within neocapitalism', but I think that it is important to point out the different cultural trends that finally flattened our social and political scene, not all of them neoliberal in origin.

The criminal justice discourse was legitimated and reinforced by its use by former 'radical' actors; this was certainly unintentional, and the consequences are being paid by these very same actors, women *in primis*. In general, this happens because the political scene becomes fragmented, political action is reduced to temporary single-issue lobbying and transversal alliances lose appeal. This is particularly the case in relation to women because they tend to be recast as especially vulnerable, susceptible to victimization, to be protected.

Victim of crime and biological citizen share their one-dimensional being, i.e., without relations if not with those who are potentially victims or 'susceptible' to develop the same illness, without history and without a past, apart from a biological one.

The individualized and privatized imperative to prevention encompasses the two, giving birth to an obsessively self-disciplining and, therefore, self-centred subjectivity where the body becomes mere material to act upon or protect. Obviously, whatever Rose says, quoting the activities of black communities lobbying for scientific research to solve their specific genetic malformations, this does produce new inequalities, inevitably added to previous ones, if only because much less attention is given to improve those general conditions which are common to all.

Simon's book makes it abundantly clear how governments, through crime, discriminate, exclude and dominate along class and race lines.

What is not said is that appeals to war (on crime, drugs, terrorism) always use a masculinist vocabulary, where the 'us' against 'them' is usually the good (white, middle-class) males called to protect 'their' belongings (women, children – the traditional family – and all other property) against the evil (other men, usually of a different skin colour and class). As I say in this book, it is the same discursive repertoire used in the case of actual war, to defend nation, country, tradition.

Simon calls this style of government authoritarian populism, which is a style of government perfectly in line with neoliberal policies, and is, in fact, their reverse side.

In Italy we have a particularly extreme example of this style, where government through crime (and fear) coexists with neoliberal discourses and, to an extent, policies.

The governing majority is indeed a mix between a xenophobic and openly racist party (*Lega*) based in the North, an ex-fascist and nationalist force and the personal party of a media tycoon, held together by a winning combination of anti-immigration propaganda (migrants are criminals and rapists) and laissez-faire policies (deregulation and dismantling of the public sector, especially the education and health systems, promises of reducing taxation, actual tolerance of tax evasion, which is endemic in Italy, all in the name of individual freedom).

The neoliberal rhetoric of individual responsibility (and freedom of choice) goes very well together with the 'us' against 'them' rhetoric supporting harsh legislation against 'illegal' migrants. Appeals to security go hand in hand with blood-and-soil, tradition, religion, all to be defended against dangerous aliens.

In all this, gender plays a fundamental role. Women's gains in the 1970s and 1980s have indeed subverted traditional gender relationships, but, even more importantly, feminism has had a vital role in the critique and crisis of traditional institutional politics, and this is especially visible in the left.

And it was actually the crisis of traditional masculinity that fuelled an imaginary where women were viewed as all powerful beings, masters of life and death (Pitch 1998). The outcries against legal abortion and legislation on assisted procreation are testimonies of a fear of women and women's freedom which was often voiced through a vocabulary of rights: the rights of fathers, embryos, foetuses. On the one hand, the rhetoric of victimization could be used to 'subjectify' foetuses against mothers; on the other hand, this same rhetoric could be used to justify prevention and repression policies against 'aliens' threatening 'our' women, thus again reducing women to vulnerable beings in need of (male) protection.

Authoritarian populism feeds on masculine fears of women and their sexuality; it uses masculinist (and frankly sexist) vocabularies to legitimate itself, all the way down to implying that the 'barbarian' hyper-sexuality of coloured foreigners is one of the main threats to 'security'. I do not think this is true only of Italy, though here this complex imagery was immensely aided by the demeaning use of female bodies in the so-called private media, owned by Berlusconi.

Yet, paradoxically, the recent scandals threatening the popularity of our prime minister were provoked by vocal women: his wife, who publicly denounced his sexual addiction and the exchange of parliamentary seats for sex; but also the prostitutes he recruited for his parties. It was their voices, rather than those of the opposition (at first prudently – and hypocritically – silent), which unveiled the weakness of a supposedly powerful male, reduced to playing this part in front of paid women. All this indeed appears a good metaphor for traditional masculinity: what the prime minister bought was not just sex, but 'admiration' (during all his parties, the women invited were subjected to long hours of viewing videos of him consorting with foreign statespersons).

I said that victim of crime and biological citizen share one significant trait, vulnerability, which is indeed their only relevant characteristic. Vulnerability, though, may be interpreted in more complex and multidimensional ways. In some recent writing, Judith Butler (2004) evokes vulnerability as precisely that fundamental human trait which might allow for a non-exclusionary political subjectivity. As all humans suffer and eventually die, the awareness of our vulnerability to pain and death could enable the recognition of our common humanity.

The ways in which victim of crime and biological citizen are the contemporary protagonists of the political and social scene is the opposite of that which Butler asks for. The victim of crime becomes a political actor via the logic and language of criminal justice, an intensely antagonistic language. Here, one's agency depends on the exclusion of 'others', rather than on the recognition of their common humanity.

The biological citizen, on the other hand, becomes a political actor on the basis of her susceptibility to the development of a particular illness or disability, thus by joining forces only with those who share that same susceptibility. In comparison with struggles to get a more efficient public health service, or cleaner air and safer work conditions, for example, this appears a rather self-centred and potentially exclusionary politics, incapable of producing a lively and transversal public realm, as this depends on sharing one's differences rather than similarities.

The body is in some sense what must be defended and/or enhanced in both cases. This is evident in the case of the biological citizen. But also the victim of crime refers to the defence of a body, conceived in Lockean terms: sovereignty over one's body means also liberty and property (one's women included in the latter).

Both bodies are far from those reclaimed by feminism. These last, as Butler's interpretation of vulnerability also shows, are at the same time what is common to all and what differentiates everybody from everybody else. They are what we are, and change as we change. They are not only biological, but historical, social, cultural bodies. They are the product of relationships and the source of relationships. A political subjectivity based on this type of bodily awareness brings on to the public realm what is common and what is different, both in biological and in social and cultural terms. It makes transversal alliances possible and useful.

It has been my contention throughout the book that the present imperative to prevention, in both its forms (self-discipline and repressive policies), reduces bodies to either biological material we must work on or to threats to 'our' safety, identity, well-being. This reduction produces a miserly and 'flattened' public realm, populated by one-dimensional actors acting mainly on the basis of fear. Indeed, it is hard to find an 'economy of hope' in this type of scenario.

Authoritarian populism thrives on fear and legitimates itself through fear. It offers 'paternal' protection in exchange for consensus, and consensus, in its turn, is used to justify a power pushing the rule of law to the limits. This is the case in Italy at present, where the leader pretends to be 'anointed' by his electoral majority and therefore constantly fights against the constitutional limitations to his power. But Italy, after all, is a democracy, part of the European Union. While this is at least in part a protection against worse developments, one may wonder if Italy's situation is only an extraordinary occurrence in a country known for its political extravagances or if it does say something about the general problems of present day democracies.

Setting aside the new democracies of Eastern Europe, some of which are going this way even more than Italy, let us look at France. On the face of it, France looks quite different from Italy. Yet, Sarkozy too uses much of the rhetoric of authoritarian populism.

The extreme right is on the rise all over Europe; explicitly xenophobic parties won quite a few seats in the most recent EU elections.

In the US, Obama's election testifies to the resilience and capacity for change in American society, and it is of course a hope for the rest of the world. But the crisis of representative democracy is well under way, and its replacement with some sort of authoritarian populism is a not improbable alternative, given the present widespread situation of 'government by fear'.

Tamar Pitch
Rome, 4 March 2010

Bibliography

Agamben, G. 1995, *Homo sacer. Il potere sovrano e la nuda vita*, Torino: Einaudi.

Agamben, G. 2003, *Stato di eccezione*, Torino: Bollati Boringhieri.

Amendola, G. 1997, *La città postmoderna*, Roma-Bari: Laterza.

Amendola, G. (ed.) 2003, *Il governo della città sicura*, Napoli: Liguori.

Appadurai, A. 1996, *Modernity at Large: Cultural Dimensions of Globalization*, Minneapolis/London: University of Minnesota Press.

Appadurai, A. 2005, *Sicuri da morire. La violenza nell'epoca della globalizzazione*, Roma: Meltemi.

Arendt, H. 1973 (1951), *The Origins of Totalitarianism*, Fort Washington, PA: Harvest Books.

Barber, B.R. 2003, *Fear's Empire: War, Terrorism and Democracy in an Age of Interdependence*, New York: W.W. Norton and Company.

Bauman, Z. 1999, *In Search of Politics*, Cambridge: Polity Press.

Bauman, Z. 2000, *Liquid Modernity*, Cambridge: Polity Press.

Bauman, Z. 2002, *Society Under Siege*, Cambridge: Polity Press.

Bauman, Z. 2004, *Wasted Lives: Modernity and its Outcasts*, Cambridge: Polity Press.

Bauman, Z. 2005, *Liquid Life*, Cambridge: Polity Press.

Beccaria, C. 2003 (1764), *Dei Delitti e Delle Pene*, Milano: Feltrinelli.

Beck, U. 1992, *Risk Society*, London: Sage.

Benasayag, M. and Schmit, G. 2004, *L'epoca delle passioni tristi*, Milano: Feltrinelli.

Berlinguer, G. 1977, Introduzione, in *La salute nelle fabbriche*, Bari: De Donato.

Bertaccini, D. 2001, *La sicurezza privata in Emilia-Romagna*, Quaderni di Cittàsicure, 7, settembre–ottobre.

Boccia, M.L. 2002, *La differenza politica*, Milano: Il Saggiatore.

Body-Gendrot, S. and Duprez, D. 2001, Les politiques de sécurité et de prévention dans les années 1990 en France, *Déviance & Société*, 4(25), 377–402.

Bonacchi, G. 2003, Il personale è impolitico: prevenzione e profiling, *DWF DonnaWomanFemme*, 4(60), 40–49.

The Boston Women's Health Collective 1973, *Our Bodies Ourselves*, Boston: The Boston Women's Health Collective.

Butler, J. 2004, *Precarious Life: The Powers of Mourning and Violence*, London/New York: Verso.

Castel, R. 2003, *L'insécurité sociale. Qu'est-ce qu'être protégé?*, Paris: Seuil.

Chambliss, B. 1999, *Power, Politics and Crime*, Boulder: Westview Press.

Cohen, S. 1985, *Visions of Social Control*, Cambridge: Polity Press.

Cosmacini, G. 1994, *Storia della medicina e della sanità nell'Italia contemporanea*, Roma-Bari: Laterza.

Crawford, A. 1999, *The Local Governance of Crime: Appeals to Community and Partnership*, Oxford: Oxford University Press.

Crawford, A. 2001, Les politiques de sécurité locale et de prévention de la délinquance en Angleterre et au Pays de Galles: nouvelles stratégies et nouveaux développements, *Déviance et Société*, 25(4), 427–458.

Dal Lago, A. 1999, *Non-persone*, Milano: Feltrinelli.

D'Avanzo, D. 2004, *Repubblica*, 3 April 2004, 32.

De Giorgi, A. 2000, *Zerotolleranza. Strategie e pratiche della società del controllo*, Roma: DeriveApprodi.

De Giorgi, A. 2002, *Il governo dell'eccedenza. Postfordismo e controllo della moltitudine*, Verona: Ombre corte.

De Giorgi, A. 2008, Introduzione all'edizione italiana, in Simon, J., *Il governo della paura*, Milano: Raffaello Cortina, XI–XXXI.

De Leonardis, O. 2001, *Le istituzioni*, Roma: Carocci.

De Martino, E. 1948, *Il mondo magico*, Torino: Boringhiere.

De Martino, E. 1959, *Sud e magia*, Milano: Il Saggiatore.

Di Bella, A. Siamo tutti sorvegliati?, in *Il Venerdì di Repubblica*, 30 June 2006, 31.

Douglas, M. 1966, *Purity and Danger*, London: Routledge & Kegan Paul.

Douglas, M. 1985, *Risk Acceptability According to the Social Sciences*, New York: Russell Sage Foundation.

Douglas, M. 1992, *Risk and Blame*, London and New York: Routledge.

Durkheim, E. 1989 (1893), *La divisione del lavoro sociale*, Torino: Comunità.

Ehrenreich, B. and English, D. 1978, *For Her Own Good: 150 Years of the Experts' Advice to Women*, New York: Anchor/Doubleday.

Felson, M. 2003, *Intervento* al convegno 'Per una società più sicura' organizzato dall'Istat, Roma, 3–5 dicembre.

Ferrajoli, L. 1989, *Diritto e ragione*, Roma-Bari: Laterza.

Ferrarese, M.R. 2002, *Il diritto al presente*, Bologna: Il Mulino.

Ferri, E. 1979 (1905), *Sociologia criminale*, Milano: Feltrinelli.

Foucault, M. 1975, *Surveiller et Punir*, Paris: Gallimard.

Foucault, M. 1984, *Le Souci de Soi*, Paris: Gallimard.

Friedman, J. 2000, Cultural Insecurities and Global Class Formation, in Tehranian, M. (ed.), *Worlds Apart. Human Society and Global Governance*, London: I.B. Tauris.

Furedi, F. 1997, *Culture of Fear*, London/New York: Continuum.

Gallerano, N. 1999, *La resistenza tra storia e memoria*, Milano: Mursia.

Garland, D. 1996, The Limits of the Sovereign State, *The British Journal of Sociology*, 36, 445–471.

Garland, D. 2001, *The Culture of Control*, Oxford: Oxford University Press.

Giovannetti, M. and Maluccelli, L. 2001, *Politiche di sicurezza e azioni di prevenzione nei comuni e nelle province della regione Marche*, relazione a cura dell' Associazione Quarz, Servizi integrati per la sicurezza, 23–24 novembre.

Glassner, B. 1999, *The Culture of Fear*, New York: Basic Books.

Harris, J. 1992, *Wonderwoman and Superman*, Oxford: Oxford University Press.

Hobbes, T. 1996 (1660), *The Leviathan*, Oxford: Oxford University Press.

Hope, T. 2003, *Intervento* al convegno 'Per una società più sicura' organizzato dall'Istat, Roma, 3–5 dicembre.

Jessop, B. 1988, *Conservative Regimes and the Transition to Post-Fordism*, Colchester: University of Essex Papers.

Jordan, B. 2002, *Gli impostori della genetica*, Torino: Einaudi.

Kaldor, M. 2006, *New & Old Wars*, Cambridge: Polity Press.

Katz, S. and Marshall, B.L. 2004, Is the Functional 'Normal'? Aging, Sexuality and the Bio-marking of Successful Living, *History of the Human Sciences*, 1(17), 53–75.

Lasch, C. 1979, *The Culture of Narcissism: American Life in an Age of Diminishing Expectations*, New York: Norton.

Latour, B. 1999, *Pandora's Hope: Essays on the Reality of Science Studies*, Cambridge, MA: Harvard University Press.

Lewontin, R. 2001, *It Ain't Necessarily So: The Dream of the Human Genome and Other Illusions*, New York: New York Review of Books.

Lianos, M. and Douglas, M. 2000, Dangerization and the End of Deviance: The Institutional Environment, *The British Journal of Criminology*, 2(40) Spring, 261–278.

Locke, J. 1987 (1690), *Two Treatises of Government*, Boston: Unwin Hyman.

Lyon, D. 2001, *Surveillance Society: Monitoring Everyday Life*, Buckingham/ Philadelphia: Open University Press.

Maccacaro, G. 1972, *Lettera all'Ordine dei medici di Milano e Provincia*, in Polack, J.-C., *La medicina del capitale*, Milano: Feltrinelli.

Madriz, E. 1997, *Nothing Bad Happens to Good Girls*, Berkeley: University of California Press.

Marconi, P. 2004, *Spazio e sicurezza*, Torino: Giappichelli.

Martinotti, G. 1993, *Metropoli. La nuova morfologia sociale della città*, Bologna: Il Mulino.

Mead, G.H. 1967 (1934), *Mind, Self and Society: From the Standpoint of a Social Behaviorist*, Chicago: University of Chicago Press.

Melossi, D. 2002, *Stato, controllo sociale, devianza*, Milano: Bruno Mondadori.

Mernissi, F. 1995, *Dreams Of Trespass: Tales Of A Harem Girlhood*, New York: Perseus Books.

Merry, S.E. 1981, *Urban Danger: Life in a Neighborhood of Strangers*, Philadelphia: Temple University Press.

Merton, R.K. 1938, Social Structure and Anomie, *American Sociological Review*, 3(5), 672–682.

Nuzzo, L. 2008, *Le anticamere del diritto. Ordine politico ed eclissi della forma giuridica*, Lecce: PensaMultimedia.

Offe, C. 1999, How Can We Trust Our Fellow Citizens?, in Warren, M.E. (ed.), *Democracy and Trust*, Cambridge: Cambridge University Press, 42–87.

Parsons, T. 1951, *The Social System*, Glencoe: Tavistock.

Pasquinelli, C. 2004, *La vertigine dell'ordine*, Milano: Baldini Castoldi Dalai.

Pateman, C. 1988, *The Sexual Contract*, Stanford: Stanford University Press.

Pavarini, M. 2001, Nota redazionale, in *La sicurezza privata in Emilia-Romagna*, Quaderni di Cittàsicure, 7, settembre–ottobre, 9–16.

Perera, S. 2006, Il genere del panico da confine, *Studi sulla questione criminale*, 1(I), 134–158.

Pitch, T. 1989, *Responsabilità limitate*, Milano: Feltrinelli.

Pitch, T. 1995, *Limited Responsibilities: Social Movements & Criminal Justice*, London and New York: Routledge.

Pitch, T. 1998, *Un diritto per due*, Milano: Il Saggiatore.

Pitch, T. 2001a, Sono possibili politiche democratiche per la sicurezza?, *Rassegna di Sociologia*, 1, 137–158.

Pitch, T. 2001b, La demoralizzazione del controllo sociale, *Iride*, 32(XIV), 103–122.

Pitch, T. 2004a, L'occultamento della politica: tra regolazione giuridica e normativa morale, *Sociologia del diritto*, 2(XXXI), 153–164.

Pitch, T. 2004b, *I diritti fondamentali: differenze culturali, disuguaglianze sociali, differenza sessuale*, Torino: Giappichelli.

Pitch, T. and Ventimiglia, C. 2001, *Che genere di sicurezza. Donne e uomini in città*, Milano: Franco Angeli.

Polanyi, K. 1957 (1943), *The Great Transformation*, Boston: Beacon Hill.

Prina, F. 2006, *Intervento* al Convegno 'Le politiche locali di sicurezza. Quale devianza, quale controllo sociale, quale politica?' a conclusione del progetto di ricerca Prin 2003, Perugia, 29–30 giugno.

Re, L. 2006, *Carcere e globalizzazione*, Roma-Bari: Laterza.

Robert, P. 2006, *Politiche di prevenzione in Europa*, relazione tenuta al convegno 'Le politiche di sicurezza. Quale devianza, quale controllo sociale, quale politica?, a conclusione del Progetto Prin 2003 sulla sicurezza urbana, Perugia, 29–30 giugno.

Rodotà, S. 2001, Prefazione, in Lyon D., *La società sorvegliata. Tecnologie di controllo della vita quotidiana*, VII–XIX, Milano: Feltrinelli.

Rodotà, S. 2006, *La vita e le regole*, Milano: Feltrinelli.

Rose, N. 2000, Government and Control, *The British Journal of Sociology*, 2(40), 321–339.

Rose, N. 2007, *The Politics of Life Itself: Biomedicine, Power, and Subjectivity in the Twenty-first Century*, Princeton: Princeton University Press.

Ruggiero, V. 2004, I vuoti delle politiche di sicurezza, in Selmini, R. (ed.), *La sicurezza urbana*, Bologna: Il Mulino, 285–294.

Sassen, S. 1994, *Cities in A World Economy*, Thousand Oaks: Pine Forge Press.

Selmini, R. 2000, Le misure di prevenzione adottate nelle città italiane, *Quaderni di Città sicure*, 11, 77–94.

Selmini, R. 2003, Le politiche di sicurezza in Italia. Origini, sviluppo e prospettive, in Barbagli, M. (ed.), *Rapporto sulla criminalità in Italia*, Bologna: Regione Emilia-Romagna, 611–648.

Selmini, R. 2004, Introduzione, in Selmini, R. (ed.), *La sicurezza urbana*, Bologna: Il Mulino, 9–22.

Selmini, R. 2006, *Intervento* al Convegno 'Le politiche locali di sicurezza. Quale devianza, quale controllo sociale, quale politica?' a conclusione del progetto Prin 2003 sulla Sicurezza Urbana, Perugia, 29–30 giugno.

Sennett, R. 1998, *The Corrosion of Character*, New York/London: W.W. Norton & Company.

Sennett, R. 2000, *The Art of Making Cities*, Conference at the London School of Economics, 9 March.

Sennett, R. 2003, *Respect: The Formation of Character in an Age of Inequality*, London: Penguin.

Simon, J. 2007, *Governing Through Crime: How the War on Crime Transformed American Democracy and Created a Culture of Fear*, Oxford: Oxford University Press.

Sociologia del diritto [Sociology of Law], XXXII, 2005(2–3).

Tönnies, F. 1979 (1897), *Comunità e società*, Torino: Comunità.

Wacquant, L. 1999, *Les prisons de la misère*, Paris: Editions Raisons d'Agir.

The White House 2002, The National Security Strategy of the United States of America, 2002. Available at http://www.whitehouse.gov/nsc/nss.html.

Wilson, J.Q. and Kelling, G.L. 1982, Broken Windows: The Police and Neighborhood Safety, *The Atlantic Monthly*, March, 29–38.

Index

Advances in Criminology

Full series list